STUMPWORK STUDIO

Mastering 3-D Embroidery

15 Realistic Nature-Inspired Projects to Stitch

MEGAN ZANIEWSKI

stashBOOKS®
an imprint of C&T Publishing

PUBLISHER | Amy Barrett-Daffin

CREATIVE DIRECTOR | Gailen Runge

SENIOR EDITOR | Roxane Cerda

EDITOR | Madison Moore

TECHNICAL EDITOR | Del Walker

COVER/BOOK DESIGNER | April Mostek

PRODUCTION COORDINATOR | Tim Manibusan

ILLUSTRATOR | Aliza Shalit

PHOTOGRAPHY COORDINATOR | Rachel Ackley

FRONT COVER PHOTOGRAPHY by Megan Zaniewski

PHOTOGRAPHY by Megan Zaniewski, unless otherwise noted

Published by Stash Books, an imprint of C&T Publishing, Inc., P.O. Box 1456, Lafayette, CA 94549

Library of Congress Cataloging-in-Publication Data

Names: Zaniewski, Megan, 1987- author

Title: Stumpwork studio-mastering 3-D embroidery : 15 realistic nature-inspired projects to stitch / Megan Zaniewski.

Other titles: Stumpwork studio-mastering 3-dimensional embroidery

Description: Lafayette, CA : Stash Books, an imprint of C&T Publishing, [2026] | Summary: "Stitch fifteen stunning three-dimensional projects with a menagerie of stumpwork embroidery and thread painting techniques! Each project includes step-by-step instructions and various techniques including beading, wire slips, felt padding, needle felting, and more that transform embroidery hoops into vibrant, sculptural art"-- Provided by publisher.

Identifiers: LCCN 2025034641 | ISBN 9781644036655 trade paperback | ISBN 9781644036662 ebook

Subjects: LCSH: Embroidery | Embroidery--Patterns

Classification: LCC TT771 .Z3625 2026 | DDC 746.44/041--dc23/eng/20250911

LC record available at https://lccn.loc.gov/2025034641

Printed in China

10 9 8 7 6 5 4 3 2 1

Dedication

To Maya, Claire, and Ian (always)

Acknowledgments

Thank you, Lee, for being my biggest supporter and strength in all things. You always believe in me, even when I'm buried under threads, edits, and self-doubt. This book exists because of your relentless encouragement.

Mom and Dad, thank you for pushing me to pursue my dreams and for providing the foundation and support needed to make it a reality.

To the incredible team at C&T Publishing: thank you for bringing this second stumpwork book to life with the same care, creativity, and enthusiasm as the first. It's a joy to work with such a skilled team that shares my love of embroidery and crafting.

A special thanks to my editor, Madison, for being so supportive and patient throughout the book writing process. I am so grateful to have you in my corner once again on this second book. Your keen and artistic attention to detail, along with your thoughtful questions, helped fine tune *Stumpwork Studio* and elevate it in a way that will certainly benefit our readers.

Thanks to Benzie Design, Colonial Needle, Jacquard Products, and Nurge for generously supplying the materials I requested to create the projects for this book. All of the products used in this book are materials I already love and use regularly in my studio, but your donations of new supplies allowed me to photograph them in their best light for our readers.

CONTENTS

INTRODUCTION

Hello, reader! I am so thankful you have picked up my book. Whether you are a beginner embroiderer or a seasoned stitcher, I hope you find this book informative and helpful in your journey.

My first exposure to embroidery came when I was very young. My grandmother and mother were both exceptionally skilled with a needle and thread. They made clothing, tapestries, quilts, and other household items. Their love of embroidery sparked my interest, but my own embroidery journey did not begin until I was a mother myself. My first attempts at embroidery were cautious at best. I tried a few small stitches on an old pillowcase, but I hesitated to attempt anything larger. I was hindered by a fear of making mistakes.

This mindset stifled my joy and creativity until I learned an important lesson: while there are best practices in embroidery, there are no rules. When you allow yourself to freely explore stitches and techniques without the worry of always doing it the "right" way, you will make creative discoveries and uncover your unique style. And while you don't need much more than fabric, needle, and thread to create beautiful designs, there is a wide world of materials to explore that can elevate your embroidery to new levels.

In my first book, *Stumpwork Embroidery & Thread Painting: Stitch 3-D Nature Motifs*, I introduced readers to simple and easy-to-learn stumpwork techniques that allow you to create realistic three-dimensional designs. With this book, I will take you beyond those stumpwork basics to cultivate an even more fun and creative approach to three-dimensional embroidery. While you can start with either title, this one explores new materials and techniques as we apply them to fifteen new nature-inspired designs. I hope that with these ideas and techniques in hand, you will gain the confidence to stitch freely and approach the creative process with playful curiosity.

I invite you to try something new, embrace your mistakes, and create something that is true to yourself. **Happy stitching!**

Stumpwork Embroidery

Stumpwork is a term that refers broadly to all three-dimensional embroidery techniques. This book covers a variety of these methods, such as padding, wire work, bead work, dimensional stitches, and fabric manipulation. The three-dimensional effect can be subtle or dramatic depending on your design and preference. Subjects can rise up from a fabric base or even stand independent of a base altogether. Stumpwork is highly adaptable and well suited to any design style or subject.

Finding Inspiration in Nature and Materials

Lean on your own experiences and observations for inspiration when choosing a subject to embroider. The more a subject interests you, the better you will become at creatively interpreting it with needle, thread, and other materials. Reference books and field guides are my go-to resources for learning about a subject. They are readily available through your local library. With practice, you will become more adept at selecting materials and fibers that are well suited to your subject.

Remember to consider unexpected materials for your stumpwork designs. Embroidery can be more than just needle and thread, and your materials do not need to be embroidery-specific to be useful. Sometimes, even simple household materials or found objects will provide a solution for that texture or shape you are trying to recreate. For example, I made the stalk of the Amanita Mushroom (page 140) from a common yet unexpected material: two tapered cork stoppers that closely resembled the sloping shape of the mushroom stalk when stacked on top of one another. Everyday items can inspire us to approach embroidery more creatively.

Thread Painting

Thread painting refers to the process of blending thread, like a painter would blend paint, to create the illusion of shadow and depth in an embroidery design. This technique is well suited to realistic designs. Long and short stitch is the primary stitch used in thread painting. The staggered lengths of this stitch allow slightly different thread colors to blend almost seamlessly into each other. I recommend working with 1 strand of thread for this stitch, as it allows you the most control over the finer details of a design, and it creates a smoother look. In addition to long and short stitch, you can work straight stitches, seed stitches, and other flat surface stitches into a design. When combined with stumpwork techniques, thread painting can bring your subject to life in an unparalleled way.

A thread-painted and stumpwork butterfly appears ready to fly from the hoop.

MATERIALS

General Embroidery Materials

Fabric

Choosing an appropriate fabric makes your stitching experience more enjoyable and yields better results. In general, look for fabric that has a tight, even weave. Fabrics with too much stretch or large, uneven weaves may distort when put in an embroidery hoop, resulting in a finished embroidery that is wrinkled or messy-looking.

COTTON

My preferred fabric for embroidery is 100% cotton. I look for a high thread count, usually 60 × 60 or 60 × 75 threads per square inch. Higher thread counts enable you to achieve greater detail in thread painting. I recommend Robert Kaufman's KONA Cotton Solids line. It is widely available in most fabric stores and online, and it comes in 365 colors, so it is easy to find the perfect shade to complement your subject.

SILK

I use two types of silk in my embroidery designs: habotai and organza. Silk habotai is a lightweight and low-sheen fabric made from 100% silk. It is smooth, semi-opaque, and it accepts dye well. I use it for silk florals and other three-dimensional fabric elements. Silk organza is a transparent and crisp 100% silk fabric. Although it is sheer, it is strong and does not tear easily like other transparent fabrics (tulle or chiffon). I use it for stumpwork projects with wire slips.

WOOL FELT

High-quality wool felt is important for padded stumpwork. Lower-quality acrylic felt tears and stretches too easily, and the rough texture can wear down more delicate threads. I recommend Benzie Design's wool-blend felt and 100% merino wool felt for padded stumpwork projects. These felts hold their shape and come in precut sheets in a wide range of colors that can easily be matched to your subject.

TEXTURED FABRICS

I use the term *textured fabric* to broadly describe fabric used to add texture or dimension to an embroidery project through appliqué. Fabrics with a high volume pile, such as fleece, velvet, or faux fur can add softness and depth to an embroidery. Vinyl is another interesting option; it comes in a wide range of colors and finishes, both smooth and textured, and does not fray. It can mimic natural, shiny surfaces such as beaks, stones, shells, claws, and scales. The sky is the limit when looking for a textured add-on fabric to match your subject.

Embroidery Hoops

I recommend beechwood embroidery hoops. My preferred brand, Nurge, makes high-quality beechwood hoops in many sizes. They hold the fabric drum tight and do not lose tension as you stitch. The smooth edges are also gentle on your hands.

Nurge also makes plastic hoops for displaying finished embroideries. Their faux-wood flexi hoops are an easy solution for giving your embroidery a beautiful framed look without the extra steps of framing.

Needles

There are a wide variety of needle types and sizes, and what you need depends on the type and size of thread you are using. I recommend needles made by John James for their precision and high quality. Each project notes a suggested needle.

EMBROIDERY

Embroidery needles are suitable for most embroidery projects with silk or cotton embroidery threads. The number of threads determines the needle size. Needles in sizes 9 and 10 are used most commonly for the projects in this book.

CHENILLE

Chenille needles are thick and sharp needles well suited for delicate and wider fibers such as chenille, silk ribbons, and wool or linen-blend threads.

BEADING

Beading needles are long, thin, and pointed. They are designed to pick up and thread even the smallest seed beads. Their longer length allows you to scoop and thread multiple beads at once.

FELTING

Felting needles come in a variety of sizes and tip shapes. I recommend a 38-gauge star-tip needle for felting padded bases, and specifically the Benzie Design line of felting needles.

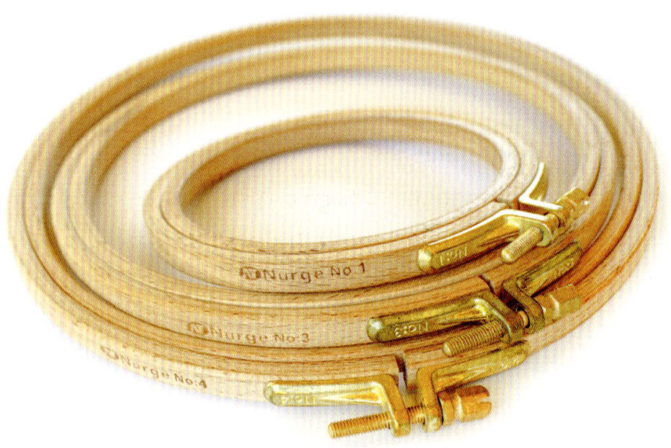

Scissors

You need two types of scissors for embroidery: fabric scissors and thread scissors. Fabric scissors are designed for cutting fabric. They are 7˝–10˝ (17.8–25.4cm) long, with a flat lower blade that glides easily along the cutting surface and leaves the cut fabric with clean edges. Thread scissors are about 3˝–4˝ (7.6–10.2cm) long, with short blades that are angled to a sharp point. They are best suited for small, precise snipping. I recommend the Karen Kay Buckley line of Perfect Scissors, especially the 4˝ (10.2cm) Multipurpose and Micro-serrated scissors.

Materials for Transferring Patterns

GRAPHITE TRANSFER PAPER

Graphite transfer paper is easy to use and accurately transfers highly-detailed designs to light and dark fabrics. Use white graphite paper for dark fabrics and black graphite paper for light fabrics. Once transferred, the design is permanent, so trace with care. See Transferring Patterns (page 23) for more on how to use graphite transfer paper.

FABRIC PENS AND PENCILS

Water- and air-soluble pens are a nonpermanent option for transferring designs onto light-colored fabrics. They are quick and easy to use, but the blunt tip on most pens is not ideal for transferring highly detailed or miniature designs.

Mechanical chalk pencils, such as Bohin's mechanical chalk pencil, can nicely transfer designs to darker fabrics. The finer tip also allows you to draw in greater detail. Chalk can sometimes rub away before you want it to, so you may need to touch up the design throughout the embroidery process.

PRINT AND STICK PAPER

C&T Publishing's Wash-Away Stitch Stabilizer and Sulky Stick 'n Stitch paper offer an effortless way to transfer designs. Simply print the design onto the water-soluble sticker paper from your home printer, peel away the sticker back, and adhere the sticker to the fabric. After you embroider the design, wash the paper away. Be sure to carefully read the paper instructions for your specific printer to ensure that the ink will not run and stain the fabric. And, always check that your thread is colorfast if you plan to use this method. See Printable Stick 'n Stitch Paper (page 24) for more on how to use this paper.

Thread

SIX-STRANDED COTTON

Six-stranded cotton embroidery floss is the most popular and accessible thread for embroidery. It comes in hundreds of colors, solid and variegated. It is made of six strands of thread that can be separated. You can stitch with all six strands for a very textured look, or you can split the thread and use fewer threads for smoother, detailed work. Most of the projects in this book require you to split the thread to just one or two strands to capture high levels of detail. When selecting cotton embroidery floss, look for high-quality, colorfast threads, such as those from DMC, Anchor, and COSMO.

SPECIALTY

I use the term *specialty thread* to refer to any threads that are not standard cotton, including metallic or iridescent threads, silk, and wool blends. These threads are often delicate and require a little more care when used in embroidery, but they can add dramatic texture and visual interest to a piece.

Frames

You can purchase new frames, or look for thrifted ones. Vintage frames often have unique characteristics that can add visual interest to a finished embroidery, and thrifted frames usually come at a lower price point. Standard store-bought frames are more widely available.

Color Wheels and Tools

A color wheel is an optional yet highly useful tool for selecting fabric and frames that perfectly complement your subject. My preferred color wheel is the C&T Publishing's Essential Color Wheel because its slotted shape allows you to easily compare fabric or paint swatches alongside it. I also recommend the 3-in-1 Color Tool by Joen Wolfrom. It offers fail-proof preset color schemes and recommendations for color groupings that take the guesswork out of selecting colors.

Hoop Stand

A hoop stand is a helpful tool that holds your embroidery hoop for you. It allows you to work two-handed stitches, like French knots and Peking knots, more easily and it helps maintain your fabric tension while you are embroidering. Hoop stands come in a variety of sizes and styles (floor, tabletop, and lap for example) so you should determine your own needs and preferences when selecting a stand. I use an adjustable lap and tabletop stand by Nurge.

Stumpwork Materials

Each project notes exactly which stumpwork materials you need, but refer back here for more details, options, and recommended manufacturers.

Beads

Wooden, wool, and cotton beads, such as Thistle Threads cotton fruit forms, come in a variety of shapes and sizes. Embroider over them with satin stitch or needle lace stitches to create three-dimensional elements such as acorns and berries.

Wire and Cutters

Use jewelry wire to create wire-slip elements that pop out from the embroidered base. A thin wire, such as 24-gauge, is easily manipulated and best used for crafting into very detailed shapes. Look for coated or rust-resistant wire that will not corrode over time. Paper-coated floral wire is well suited for thread-wrapping. I use a mix of 30-, 26-, and 18-gauge floral wires for thread-wrapped designs. You will also need wire cutters to trim the wire. The Cousin D.I.Y. 3-in-1 Tool from Benzie Design combines a wire cutter with a useful plier tip for gripping and forming wires into precise shapes.

Thread Conditioner

Strengthen and smooth embroidery floss that is wrapped around wire slips with a beeswax thread conditioner. The conditioner prevents tangling and fraying. Beeswax is also used to stiffen cotton string for padded stumpwork.

Mini Iron

A mini iron is a useful tool for shaping fabric that has been treated with fabric stiffeners. The Clover Mini Iron II comes with a spade-shaped attachment that can be used to iron realistic details, such as the veins of a leaf, onto silk florals and other natural designs.

Padded Filling

WOOL

I recommend 100% wool roving for stumpwork padding and slips. I use core wool roving and Corriendale wool roving from Benzie Design in the book projects.

FILLING ALTERNATIVES

Poly-fil Fiber Fill and spun cotton roving are hypoallergenic alternatives to wool. They do not felt as well as wool, but they can be used as a good substitute for filling.

Glues and Fabric Stiffeners

I use fabric glue to secure the edges and backside of a wire-slip embroidery and to adhere thread and fabric elements to wire. Aleene's Fabric Fusion and Beacon Fabri-Fix are my preferred fabric glues. I use fabric stiffeners like Plaid Stiffy and Jacquard Fabric Sculpting Medium to create three-dimensional fabric elements, such as silk florals.

Dyes, Paints, and Pastels

Jacquard Textile paint and Green Label Silk Dyes are my preferred mediums for painting and dyeing fabric. Pan Pastels and other art supplies such as colored pencils, oil pastels, and Caran D'Ache Neocolor pastels are also great ways to color on fabric that has been treated with a fabric stiffener. Pastels will smudge if they are handled too much, so apply a clear spray fixative, such as Krylon Workable Fixatif, to seal and protect the color.

DISPLAYING EMBROIDERY

Frame Selection

Framing should never be an afterthought. Instead, think of frames as an extension of the artwork itself. In a stumpwork design, a well-suited frame can make the three-dimensional features stand out. Your subject will appear more life-like as it "breaks the frame." Selecting a frame before you begin embroidering also makes a big difference in creating a beautifully finished, cohesive design.

Frame Size

Before you start embroidering, consider how the design will look in its final frame. The embroidery should be centered with enough negative space to ensure it is not over-crowded. A frame that is too large can overwhelm your stumpwork project, and the dimension and depth of your work will be lost. A too-small frame can disturb the visual balance of a design and make your work appear awkwardly sized. Be sure that three-dimensional features, such as moth wings or flower petals, overlap the edge of the frame only slightly, about 1˝ (2.5cm) or less for the most balanced look.

Frame Color

Choose frames that have matching or complementary colors to the dominant colors in your design and background fabric. Alternatively, neutral wood and gold-tone frames work well with most designs.

• PICKING COMPLEMENTARY COLORS •

A color wheel is an easy and fail-proof tool for selecting complementary colors. I recommend Joen Wolfrom's Essential Color Wheel Companion.

Paper Models

I make three-dimensional paper models of my designs to help visualize how a finished embroidery will look in a frame. Simply print the pattern, cut it out, and glue or tape the parts together to create the model. Place the paper model in different frames to see which style best suits the design. This step can also help you adjust the scale of the design as needed. Try out different frames. It will take some practice, but soon you will begin to spot which frame features work well with your designs.

TOO SMALL

This frame is too small for the subject. The butterfly's wings overlap half of the frame's edges, and there is not enough negative space around the butterfly's body. The shape makes the butterfly appear uncomfortably boxed in. ▶

TOO LARGE

The frame's oval shape complements the butterfly's long body shape, but the dimensions are too large. The excess of negative space around the butterfly makes the three-dimensional wing effect appear underwhelming. ▼

JUST RIGHT

There is a balance of negative space around the butterfly's body, and the wings just barely overlap the edges of the frame. The oval shape complements the subject's elongated body and outstretched antenna. The colors of the frame's mosaic tiles pair well with the butterfly's pale lavender coloring. ▼

Displaying in a Hoop

A hoop is the simplest way to display a finished embroidery. You may need to use a different size hoop than the one you used while embroidering. Some hoops, such as Nurge Flexi hoops, are suitable only for display and not for stitching, but they offer a more finished look.

1. Center and secure the embroidery in the hoop. Gently pull the fabric drum tight so the embroidery is wrinkle-free. Trim away the excess fabric so only a 1¼˝ (3.2cm) border remains.

2. Measure and cut a piece of size 8 pearl cotton embroidery thread (any color) about 3˝ (7.6cm) longer than the length of the hoop's perimeter. Thread a chenille needle with it and knot the end.

3. On the backside of the hoop, bring the needle through the middle of the excess fabric. **A**

4. Make a ⅜˝ (1cm) straight stitch through the excess fabric. **B**

5. Continue to make evenly spaced ⅜˝ (1cm) running stitches along the perimeter of the hoop until you're back at the beginning. **C**

6. Gently pull the excess thread to gather the fabric. **D**

7. Knot and trim the excess thread. **E-F**

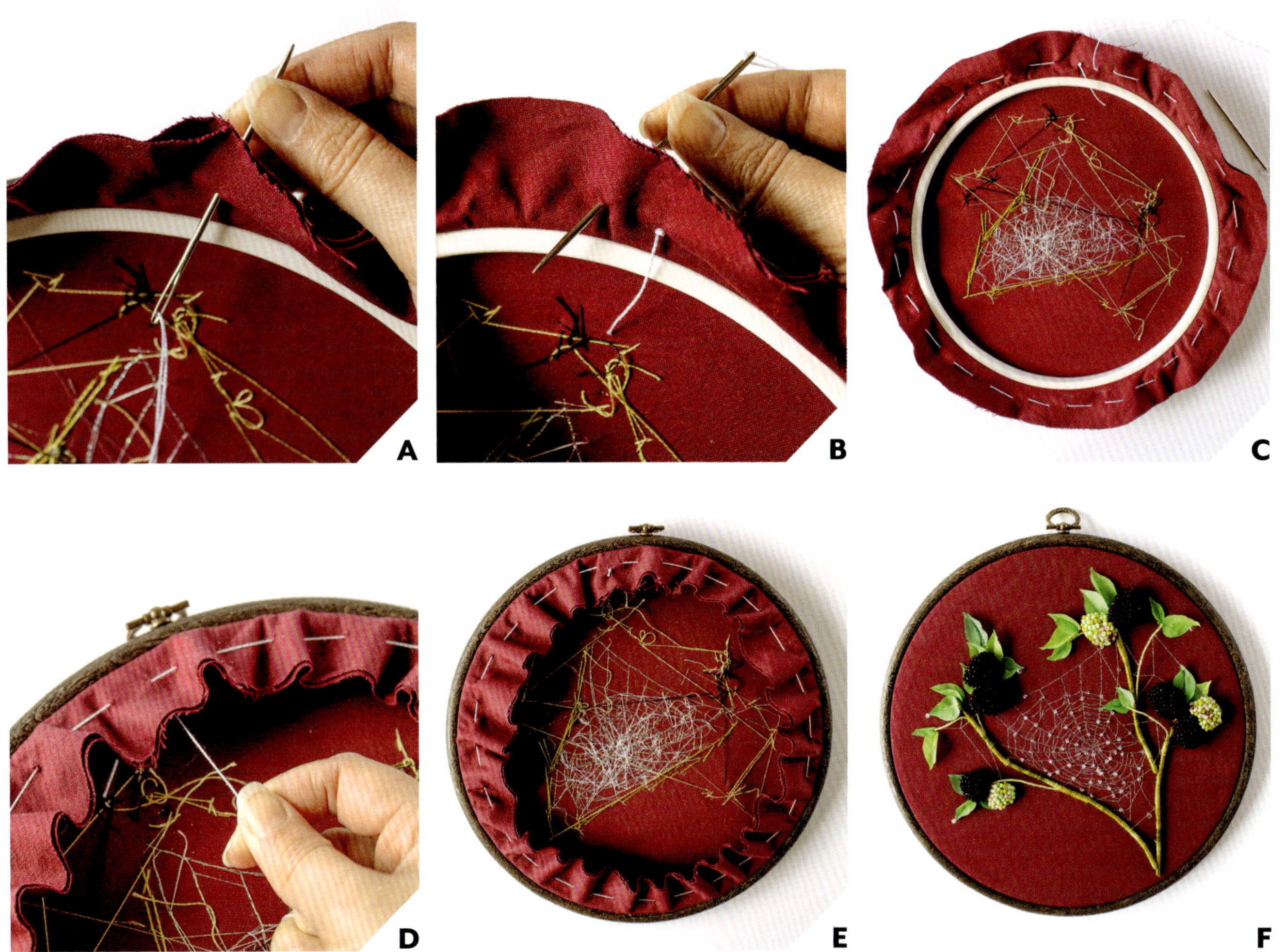

Displaying in a Frame

You need an acid-free archival mat board.

1. Cut a piece of acid-free archival mat board to fit inside the frame. Trim away the excess fabric, leaving a 1½˝ (3.8cm) margin around the design. **A**

2. Measure and cut a piece of pearl cotton embroidery thread (any color) twice the length of the perimeter of the mat board. Thread a chenille needle with it. Stitch a ⅜˝ (1cm) running stitch around the embroidery, about ⅝˝ (1.6cm) from the edge. Leave the excess thread attached to the needle and fabric. Press the mat board onto the back of the embroidery. **B**

3. Hold the mat board in place. Gently pull the excess thread to gather the fabric around it. **C**

4. Push the needle between the fabric and mat board at any point along the perimeter. **D**

A

B

C

D

5. Bring the thread across the back of the board to the opposite side and pull the needle through. Repeat in both directions until the backside is crisscrossed with thread. Gently pull the fabric taut with each pass of the needle. This will help flatten the back of the fabric. Tie off the end of the thread. **E**

6. Place the embroidery into the frame and ensure that the design is centered and wrinkle-free. **F**

7. Attach the backing board of the frame.

E

F

STITCHES AND BASIC TECHNIQUES

Transferring Patterns

Graphite Transfer Paper

Graphite transfer paper is my preferred method for transferring designs. Black graphite paper is suitable for lighter fabrics, and white graphite paper is suitable for darker fabrics. One sheet of graphite paper can be used multiple times before losing its effectiveness. The downside to this method is that the pattern lines cannot easily be removed from the fabric. Your stitches will need to cover the pattern completely so that the lines are not visible. If you do make a mistake when transferring the design, Amodex Ink and Stain Remover can remove the graphite lines from most fabrics.

1. Tape the fabric right side up on a flat, hard surface. Place a piece of graphite paper over the fabric with the graphite side facing down. Place the printed pattern over the graphite paper. **A**

2. Slowly trace each line in the pattern with a fine-tipped pen. Use enough pressure to transfer the design clearly, but do not rip the paper. **B**

3. Remove the tape and graphite paper. Check for any mistakes. The pattern is ready to be embroidered. **C**

• LAYERING FABRIC •

Many fabrics, even high-quality quilting cottons, are semi-transparent. I like to add an extra layer of fabric behind the transferred pattern and secure both pieces in the hoop together to create a fully opaque background. This second layer will help hide the reverse side of the embroidery and deepen the fabric to its full, rich color. A second layer of fabric also provides better fabric tension by filling the gap more completely between the inner and outer embroidery hoops.

A

B

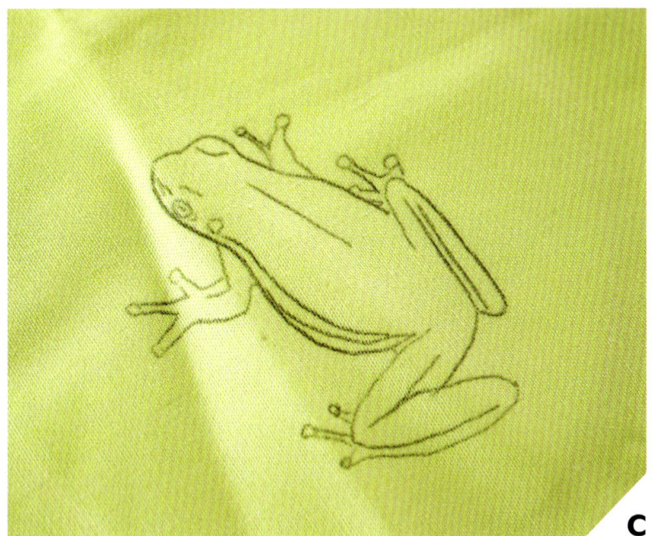

C

Printable Stick 'n Stitch Paper

C&T Publishing's Wash-Away Stitch Stabilizer and Sulky Stick 'n Stitch paper provide a quick and easy way to transfer designs. Keep in mind that this transfer method works only with colorfast threads (that do not run when washed), such as DMC, COSMO, and Anchor. This paper can be used with most fabrics.

• STICKY STABILIZER CONCERNS •

Sometimes sticker-based stabilizers lose their stickiness due to handling or changes in the humidity. You can use a temporary running stitch around the margin of the stabilizer to better secure the design in place. Once the design is embroidered, simply cut away the running stitch and wash the stabilizer as usual.

• TRANSFERRING PATTERNS TO TRANSPARENT FABRIC •

Washable stitch stabilizer is my preferred method for transferring designs to transparent fabrics such as silk organza. Transparent fabrics do not accept other transfer methods as well as cotton or linen. An added benefit to using this method with a delicate fabric is that the paper provides more stability.

1. Follow the package instructions to print the design onto the sticker paper with your home printer. Cut around the design, leaving a ½″–1″ (1.2–2.5cm) margin. Secure the fabric in the hoop and tighten the hoop's hardware until the fabric is drum-tight. **A**

2. Peel away the back of the sticker and adhere it to the fabric. **B**

3. Embroider the pattern. After the project is complete, hand wash the paper away in warm, soapy water. Rinse well and air-dry.

A

B

Splitting Six-Stranded Thread

A 6-stranded cotton embroidery thread is divisible, which means that it is made up of separate individual threads wound together. Most patterns in this book require you to split the stranded thread down to one or two strands.

To split the threads, gently hold all the threads between two fingers. With your other hand, isolate a single thread and slowly pull it up. The thread should slide free of the other strands without tangling.

Stitches

The stitches in this section are used in the projects throughout the book. Refer to this section as needed.

Straight Stitch

Keep straight stitches short, no longer than ⅜" (1cm). Multiple straight stitches with spaces in between are called *running stitches*.

1. Bring the needle up through the fabric from back to front at the starting point of the stitch. **A**

2. Bring the needle back down through the fabric to create the stitch. **B**

Seed Stitch

Seed stitches are embroidered the same way as straight stitches. The difference between the two stitches is the length. Seed stitches are much smaller, usually only 1 or 2 millimeters long.

1. Follow the instructions for Straight Stitch (left), but make the stitch smaller. **C**

A

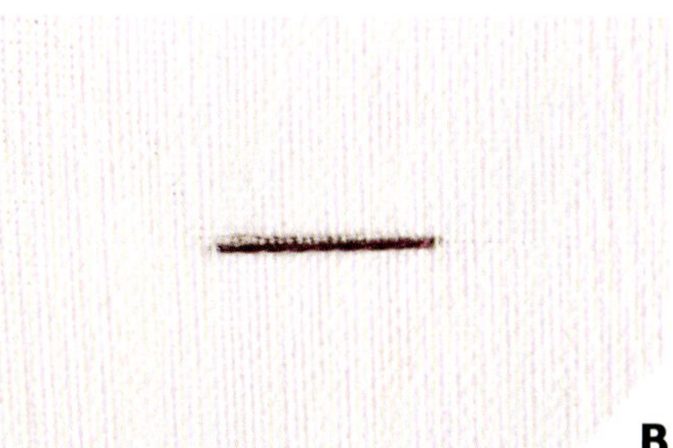

B

A cluster of seed stitches at various angles

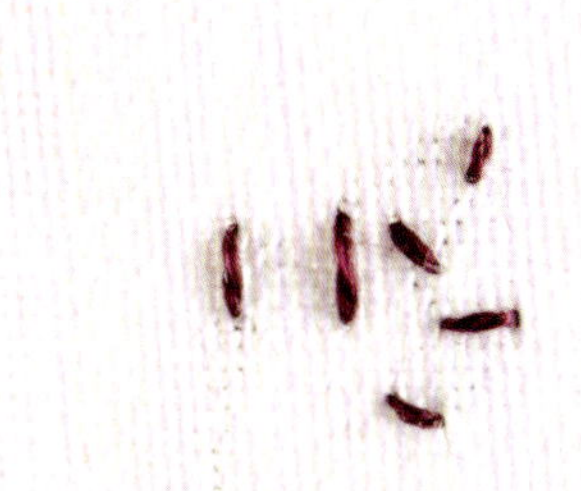

C

Back Stitch

Backstitches are embroidered with a series of equal-length, connected straight stitches.

1. Make a straight stitch. **A**

2. Bring the needle back up through the fabric a stitch-length away from the end of the first stitch. Come down again through the same hole where the first stitch ends. **B**

3. Repeat Steps 1–2 until you have completed the line of stitches. **C**

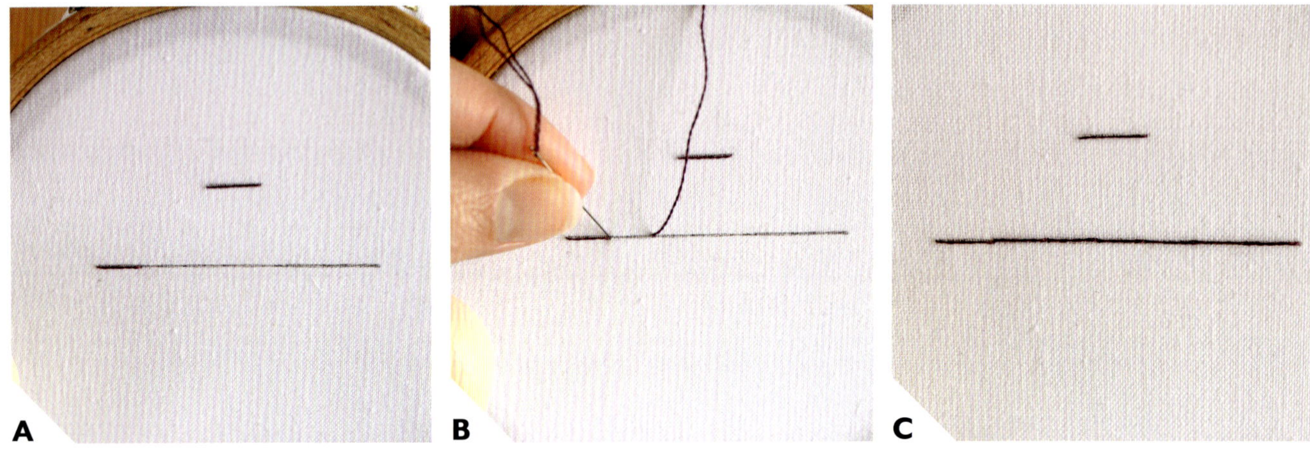

A B C

Split Stitch

For thick lines, use an even number of strands so that the stitch appears symmetrical. For very fine lines, use only 1 strand and split the thread evenly.

1. Make a straight stitch. Bring the needle back up through the fabric in the middle of the straight stitch, splitting the threads. **D**

2. Bring the needle down a stitch length away. **E**

3. Repeat Steps 1–2 until you have completed the line of stitches. **F**

D E F

French Knot

The trick to embroidering French knots with ease is maintaining tension on the thread. Hold the needle with one hand, and gently grip the working thread with the other to create even tension.

1. Bring the needle up through the fabric at the point where you want the finished knot to be. Drape the thread over the needle. **A**

2. Wrap the thread around the needle once for a small knot. For larger knots, wrap the thread around the needle multiple times. **B**

3. Keeping tension on the working thread, bring the needle down through the fabric, right next to the starting point. **C**

4. Pull the thread all the way through to form the knot. **D**

· HOOP STAND ·

A hoop stand is one of my favorite and most used tools for embroidery. It makes two-handed stitches, such as French knots, much easier to manage. Another benefit is that it can alleviate hand strain by freeing your hands from gripping the hoop. Finally, it also can help maintain your fabric tension while you embroider.

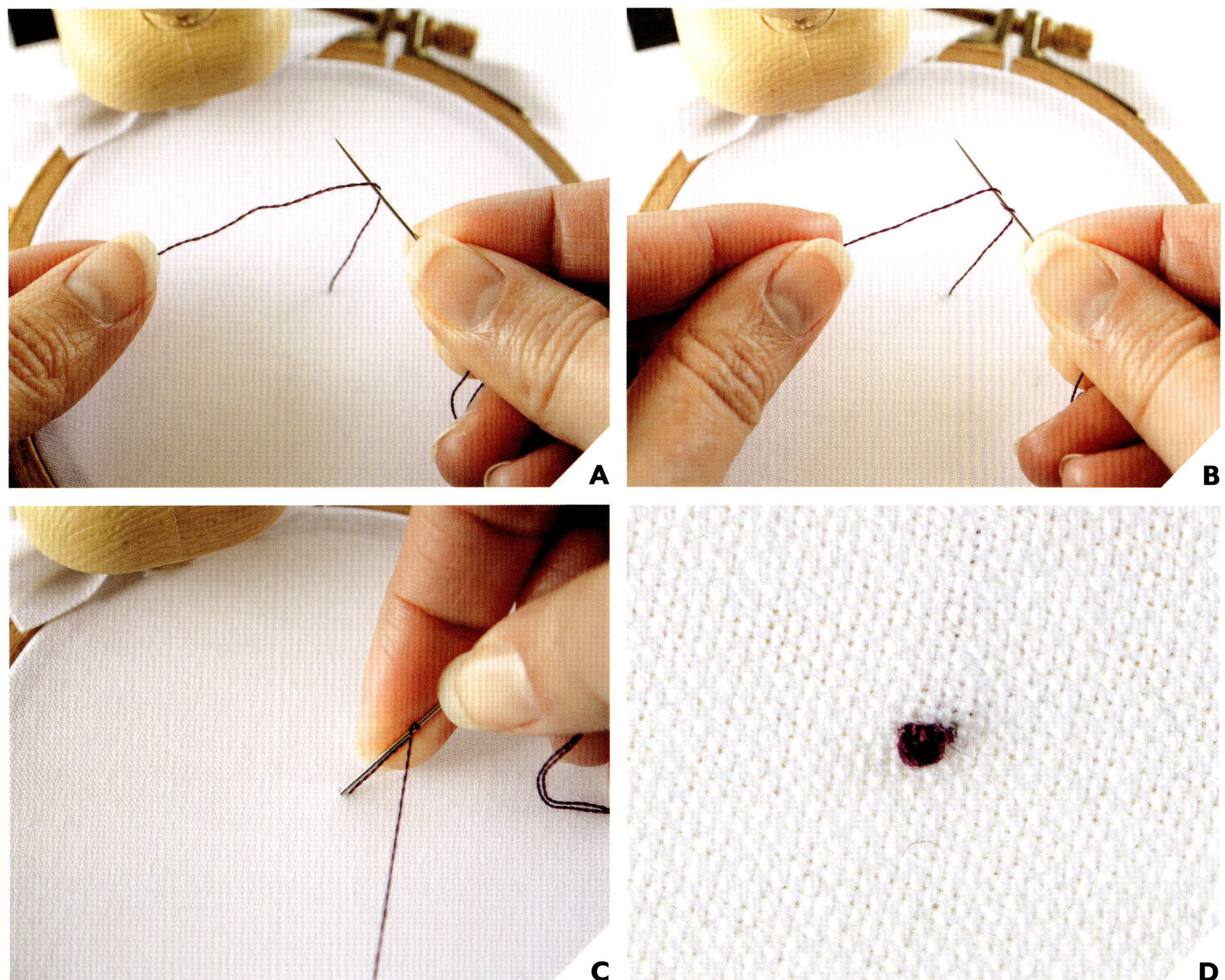

Peking Knot

A Peking knot is a loop of thread anchored by a knot. The loop lays flat against the fabric.

1. Bring the needle up through the fabric at the point where you want the top of the loop to be anchored. Shape a loop with the thread close to the starting point. **A**

2. Bring the needle through the loop of thread and back down through the fabric next to the starting point. **B**

3. Gently pull the thread to finish the anchoring stitch. Do not pull too hard, or the loop of thread will be pulled through the fabric as well. **C**

The size of the thread loop in Step 1 determines the final size of the stitched loop.

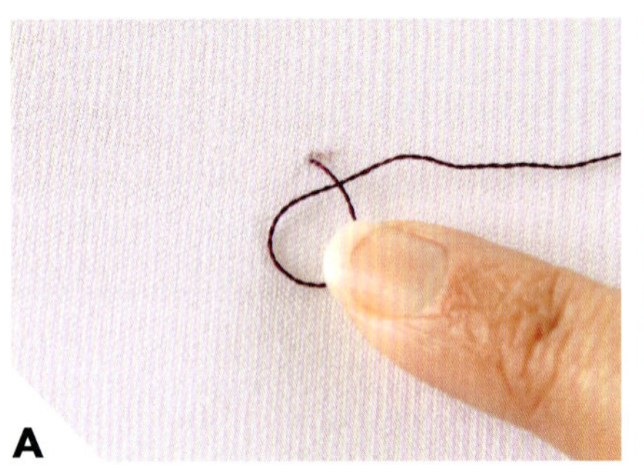
A

B

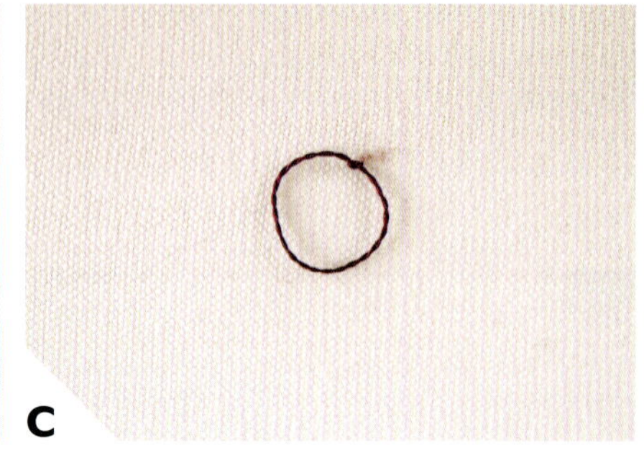
C

Satin Stitch

Satin stitches fill an entire area with thread.

1. Bring the needle up at the top right edge of the area to be filled. **D**

2. Bring the needle down through the fabric directly across from the starting point, creating a straight stitch. **E**

3. Repeat Steps 1–2 until the shape is filled. Keep the stitches close together so there are no gaps between them. Change the length of the stitch as needed to fit the shape. **F**

THREAD GRAIN

Thread has a directional grain, which is the direction the thread's fibers lay. Alternating the grain direction of the thread can make satin stitches look rougher. When filling a shape with satin stitch, bring the needle up on one side of the shape and back down directly across from it. The thread should then cross the backside of the fabric so that your next stitch starts on the same side the first stitch started. In other words, do not start the second stitch on the same side that you ended the first stitch. Beginning the stitches on the same side each time ensures that your thread's grain is consistent across the stitched area. Your stitches will appear more smooth and neat as a result.

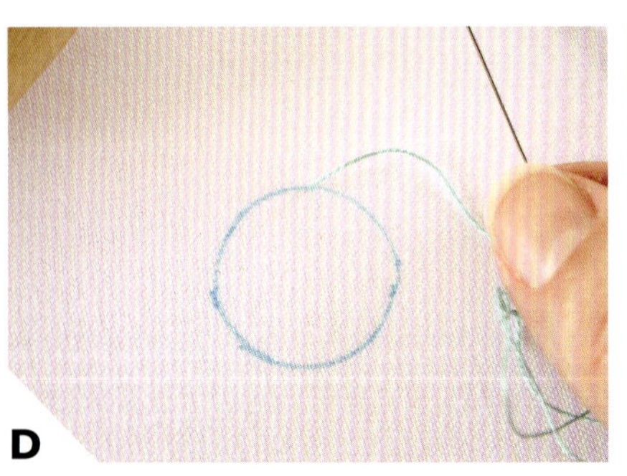
D

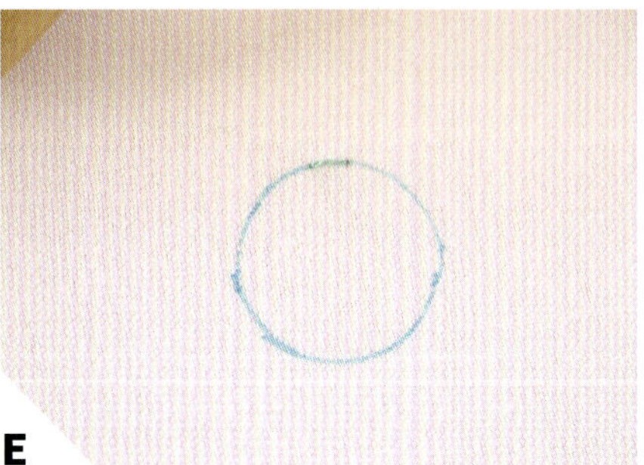
E

F

Turkey Stitch

The turkey stitch, or Ghiordes knot, is a three-dimensional stitch that creates a fluffy texture. When embroidering this stitch, I often thread my needle with two shades from the same color family to create extra depth.

1. Bring the needle up at the top edge of the area to be filled. **A**

2. Bring the needle down directly next to the starting point. Do not pull the thread all the way through. Leave a loop of thread about ⅝″–⅞″ (1.6–2.2cm) tall on the front side of the work. **B**

3. Bring the needle up between the two points of the loop. **C**

4. Bring the needle down to the right side of the loop. **D**

5. Pull the thread all the way through to create an anchor stitch at the right base of the loop. **E**

6. Repeat Steps 1–5 directly next to the first loop. **F**

7. Continue to repeat Steps 1–5 to fill the shape with rows of anchored loops. **G**

8. Cut through the loops at the top. Trim the threads to the desired height and shape for the project. Gently rub the threads with your finger or a dry, clean bristle brush to fluff and loosen them. **H**

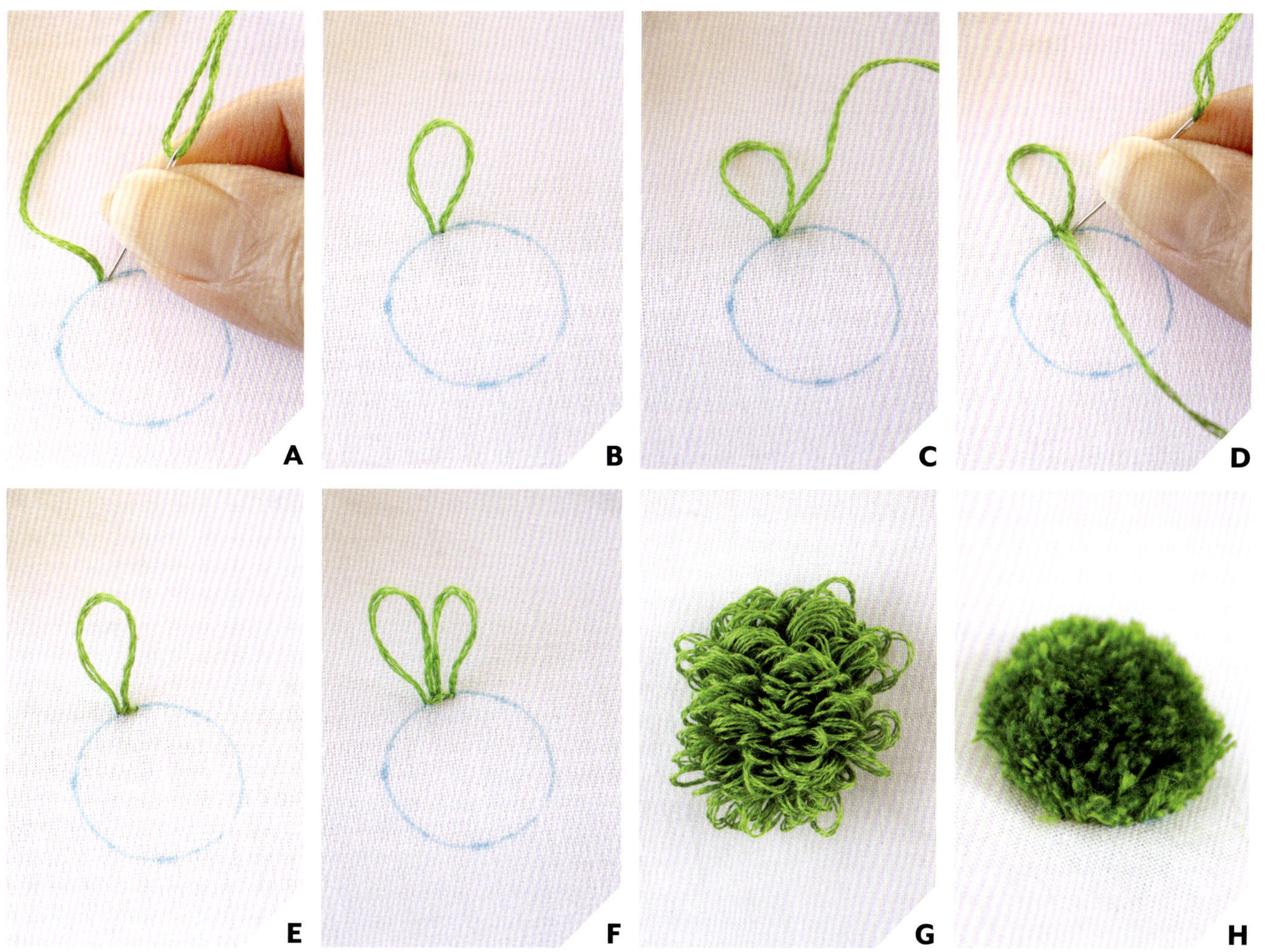

Couch Stitch

In this book, couching stitches are used to secure cording, wire slips, felt padding, and fabric applique to a base fabric. This tutorial models how to couch stitch along the edge of a piece of felt padding. When working with materials that you cannot stitch through, such as wire or cording, the couching stitches should begin and end on either side of the wire or cording as close as possible. See Stumpwork Techniques (page 32) for more information.

1. Place the felt piece (or other stumpwork add-on) onto the base fabric. Bring the needle up through the fabric and felt layers, about 5mm from the edge of the felt piece. **A**

2. Bring the needle down directly outside the edge of the felt piece through only the fabric layer. Pull the thread through, creating a straight stitch. **B**

3. Repeat Steps 1–2 around the edge of the felt piece until it is anchored in place. The stitches should be about 5mm apart. **C**

A B C

Long-and-Short Stitch

Long-and-short stitches are the foundation of thread painting. You can smoothly blend different thread colors by embroidering rows of stitches of varying lengths. Keep stitches ½" (1.2cm) or shorter.

1. Begin at one end of the area to be filled. I usually begin with the darkest shade in the gradient. Create a row of neatly aligned stitches that alternate between long and short. **A**

2. Embroider a second row of alternating long-and-short stitches in the second color. Fill in any gaps left by the short stitches of the first row, creating a second row of varied lengths. **B**

3. Blend a third row of long-and-short stitches into the second row with the third color. **C**

4. Continue to fill in the remaining area with rows of long-and-short stitches. The stitches in the final row are different lengths, but they all end at the same point. **D**

· FILL COLOR ·

Long and short stitch is useful for filling areas with a smooth and well-blended look. This tutorial blends several colors together, but you can also fill an area with long-and-short stitches of just one color.

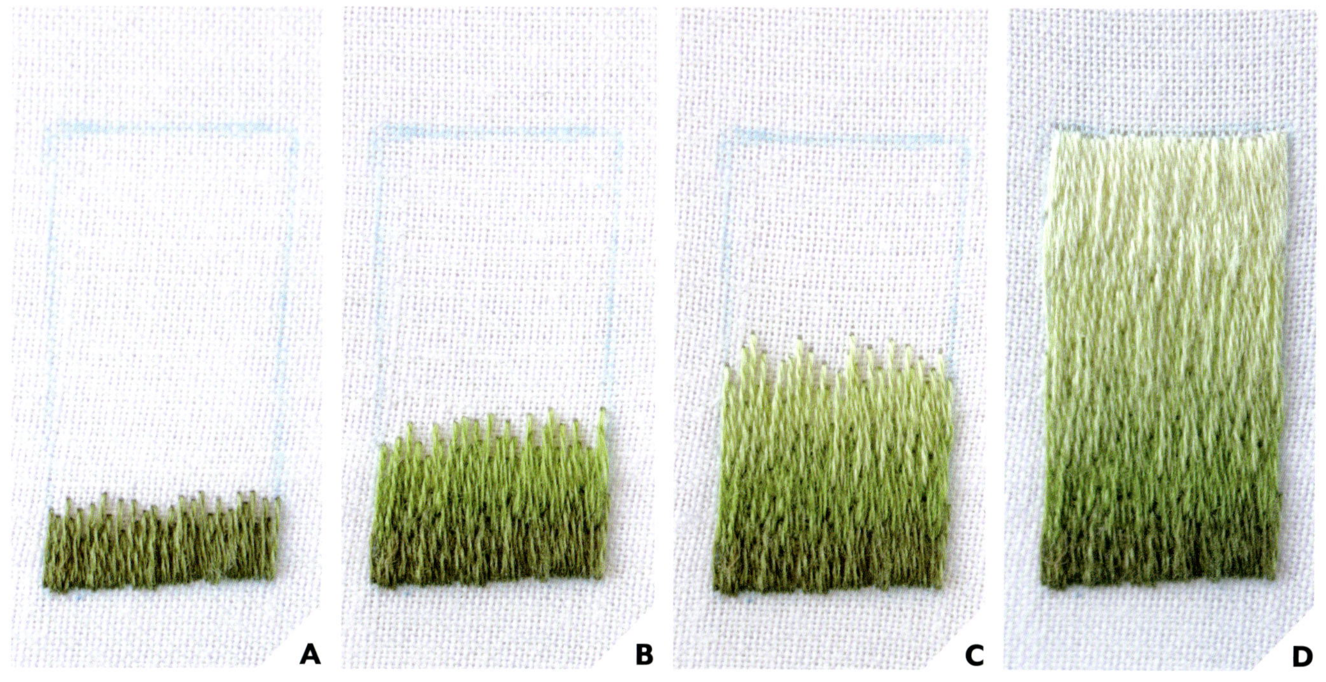

STUMPWORK TECHNIQUES

Stumpwork embroidery includes a wide variety of stitches, techniques and materials that add three-dimensional volume and texture to designs. This chapter does not cover all the available methods and materials under the broad umbrella of stumpwork embroidery. Rather, I selected some of the most versatile and accessible techniques that can elevate designs with both subtle and dramatic effects. The techniques covered in this section should inspire you to consider how thread and materials can be manipulated in creative ways to bring a subject to life in realistic detail.

Padding

Padded stumpwork is the process of layering material to a fabric base, forming a raised shape to embroider over. This technique adds depth and dimension to an embroidered subject.

Felt Padding

Felt padding is the process of layering felt pieces to a fabric base. Felt pieces are stitched over each other in slightly increasing size to build up the form. Be sure to use a felt color that matches the subject you're embroidering.

1. Begin by cutting out a piece of felt in the shape that you want to embroider. Cut out increasingly smaller pieces of felt in the same shape. Each felt shape should be approximately 1cm smaller than the one before it. **A**

2. Couch stitch the *smallest* felt piece to the fabric base with a matching thread color. **B**

3. Layer the next largest felt piece over the first piece. Couch stitch it to the fabric. **C**

4. Repeat Step 3 with the largest felt piece. **D**

· NUMBER OF LAYERS ·

The number of felt layers determines the height of the padding. This model demonstrates how subtle depth can be created with just three felt pieces. You can add more felt layers for a more dramatic three-dimensional effect.

A

B

C

The padded base is now ready to be embroidered.

D

Needle-Felted Padding

Needle-felted padding is another way to build up a three-dimensional base to embroider on top of. In contrast to felt layers, needle-felted padding can achieve greater and more varied depth across the shape. This tutorial will model how to use a barbed felting needle to poke into wool fibers, causing them to adhere to a fabric base. As you continue to add wool fiber and to felt it with the needle, the shape will become taller and more firm.

ROUND SHAPES

1. Place the base fabric (in the hoop) over a felting pad. Begin with a pinch of wool roving. Hold the felting needle straight down, and poke the roving into the center of the shape. Continue felting the wool by poking straight down repeatedly until the wool adheres to the fabric and a smooth padded form takes shape. **A**

2. Continue adding roving to fill in the shape to the desired height. Define the edges of the felted base by carefully tucking stray fibers inward with the felting needle. **B**

3. Poke the felt repeatedly until the base is firm. The embroidery will not lay smoothly over the felted base if it is not firm. Use small pointed scissors to trim away any flyaway fibers. **C**

A B C

NARROW SHAPES

1. Pinch off a small piece of roving and roll it between your fingers to form a rope-like shape. **D**

2. Begin at one end of the shape and felt the roving in place by poking it repeatedly with the needle until the wool adheres to the fabric. With your other hand, gently pull the roving to keep its narrow form. **E**

3. Felt the roving until it is firm, adding thin pieces of felt if needed, until the shape is filled to the desired height. **F**

D E F

String Padding

Cotton string or cotton yarn, can create a firm and dense padded base. Bernat Handicrafter cotton solid yarn is my preferred string for this type of padding. It is divisible, so you can remove threads to fill narrow shapes if needed. Alternatively, you can bundle multiple pieces of string together to fill larger shapes or add more height to the padding.

1. Run the string through a beeswax thread conditioner several times until it is smooth and stiffer. **A**

2. Couch stitch the string every ⅜″ (1cm) with 1 strand of regular cotton embroidery thread in the desired shape. **B**

3. Begin at one end of the string. Couch stitch over the string padding with your preferred thread. **C**

4. Continue couch stitching over the string padding until it is covered. **D**

Contrasting thread color for visibility

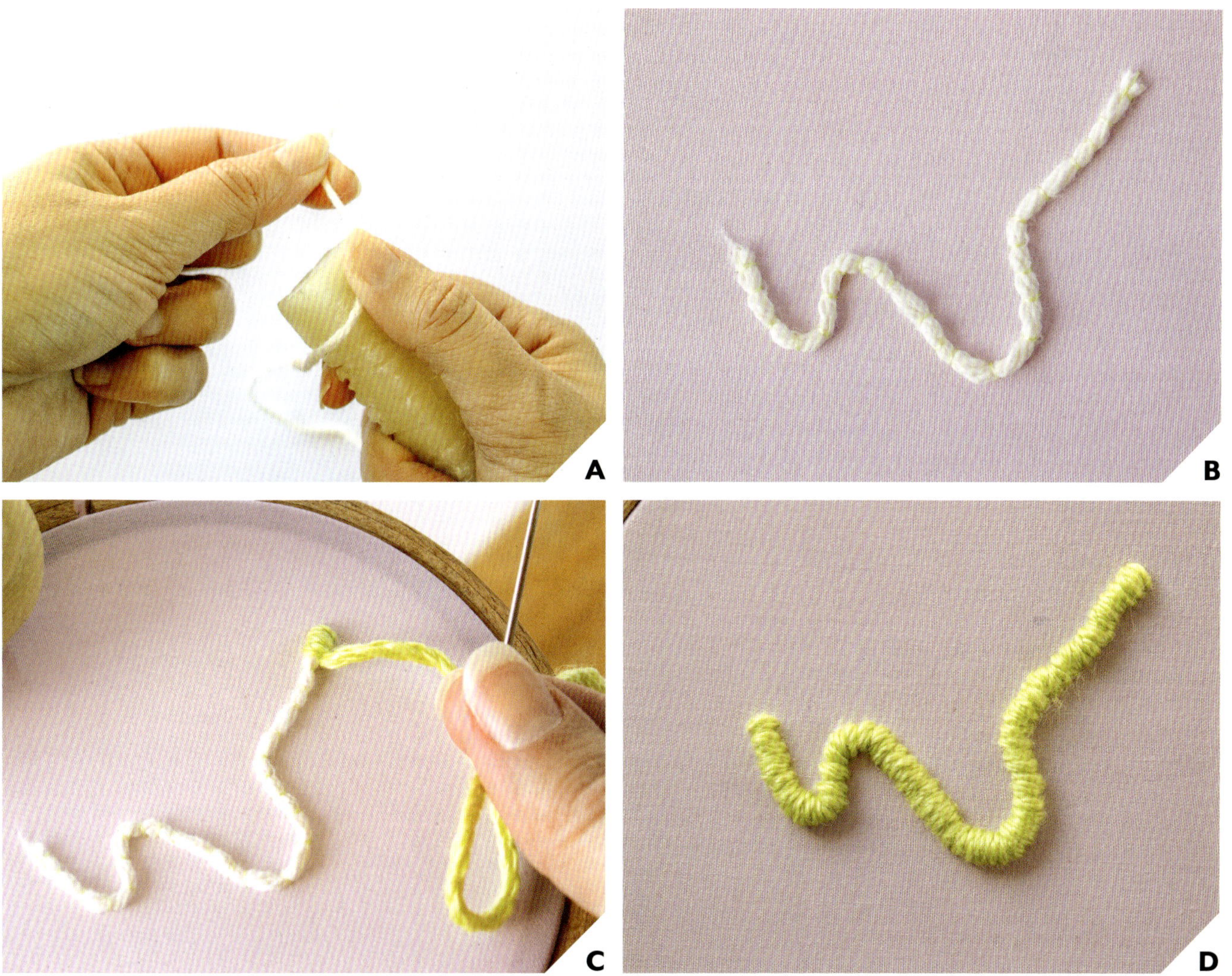

Wires

Use wire to add structural, free-standing features to an embroidery design.

Thread-Wrapped Wires

Wrap wires with thread to create botanical elements, such as vines, stems, and roots, or animal features, such as antennae and legs. Paper-coated floral wire works best for this method. The paper provides necessary friction that helps prevent the thread from slipping. Once the wire is wrapped, twist it into the desired shape.

SINGLE WIRE

1. Run the wire across a white craft glue stick to help the thread adhere more easily. **A**

2. Cut a length of thread long enough to wrap the wire. Place one end of the thread along the wire. **B**

3. Hold the thread in place between two fingers. With your free hand, wrap the thread around the wire, starting at one end of the wire and enclosing the thread end. **C**

4. Continue to wrap the wire until the desired length is covered with thread. Use multiple thread colors as desired. **D**

5. Tie a knot around the wire. Repeat with a second knot to secure it in place. Trim the excess thread. **E-F**

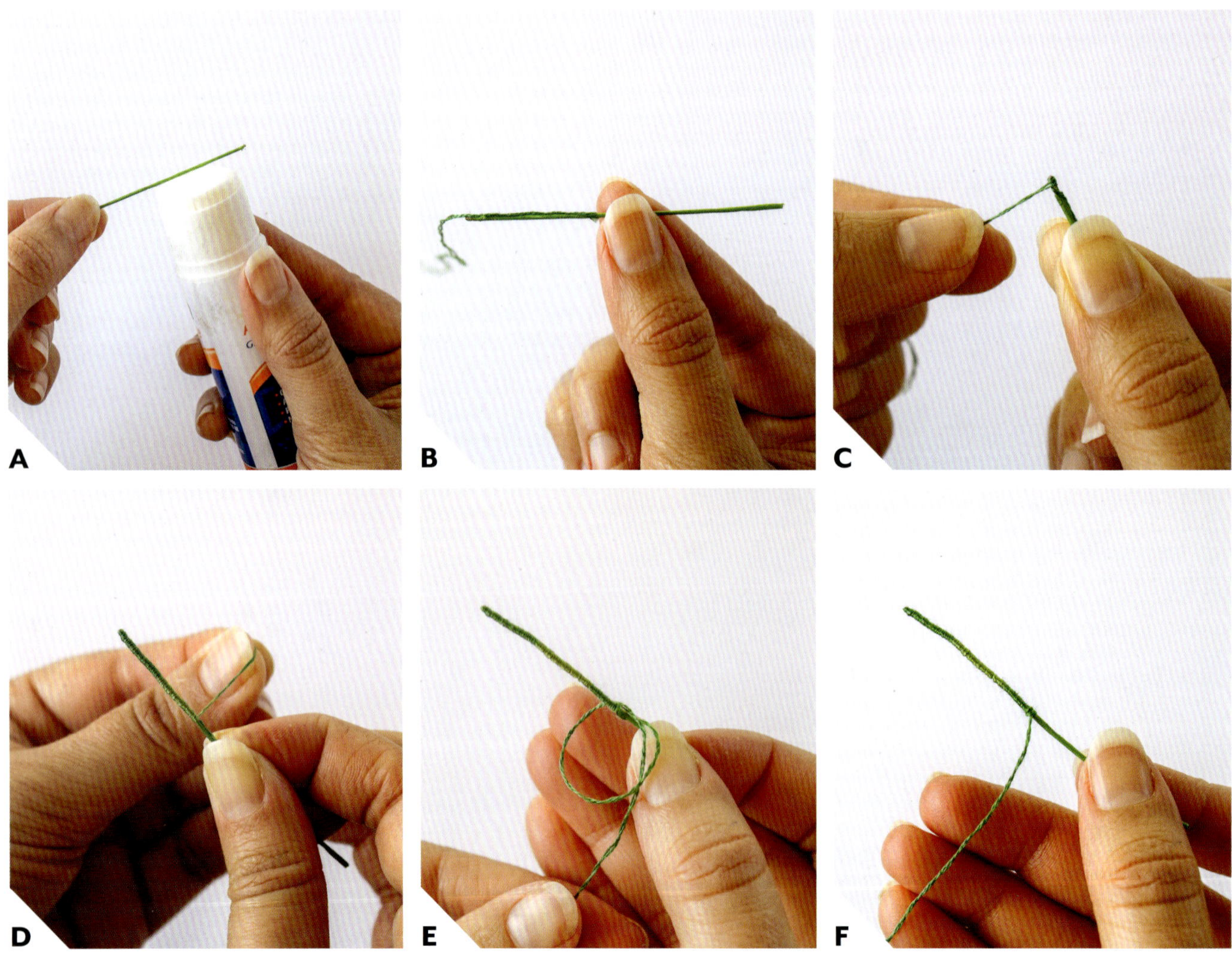

BRANCHED WIRES

Wrap multiple thread-wrapped wires together to form branching designs. You can use the same gauge wire for all the branches or mix gauge sizes for more variety. Always wrap the branches first before attaching them to the main stem. Use the single-wire method described at left to create each branch and then attach them to the stem using the tutorial below.

1. Wrap the individual branch or branches separately. Use the tutorial for wrapping single wires (left). Set the wrapped wires aside.

2. Begin to wrap the stem. Follow Steps 1–3 for wrapping a single wire (left). Stop wrapping the wire when you want to add on a branch. **A**

3. Line up the already-wrapped branching wire next to the main (stem) wire. **B**

4. Hold the wires together with one hand. Continue to wrap the thread around both wires with your free hand until both wires are secure. **C**

5. Wrap the remaining (stem) wire and tie off the ends. Trim away the excess thread. **D**

Wire Slips

Wire slips create a framework to support an embroidered design so that it can stand upright, either attached to a fabric base or on its own. The wire gives the embroidery structure and prevents the design from fraying once it is cut. Always select a fabric base that closely matches the color of the thread used to wrap the wire slip, or embroider on a transparent fabric like silk organza instead. Otherwise, you will end up with a visibly distracting "halo" of fabric around the cut edges of the design.

1. Run the thread through a beeswax thread conditioner. **A**

> **• THREAD CONDITIONER •**
> *Thread conditioner strengthens thread and prevents it from breaking or fraying during the couching process.*

2. Cut a piece of jewelry wire long enough to go around the shape with an additional 2" (5.1cm) excess. Begin 1" (2.5cm) below the design and place the wire alongside the edge of the design. **B**

3. Bring the needle up on one side of the wire and back down directly across on the other side of the wire to complete the first couch stitch. **C**

4. Repeat Step 3 with couch stitches spaced 1cm apart, bending the wire as you go, until the shape is outlined in wire and the wire ends meet at the bottom. Twist the excess wire ends together. **D**

5. Begin on the right side. Continue the couch stitches around the wire, covering it. Place each stitch directly next to the last so there are no gaps between the stitches. Cover the wire completely. **E-F**

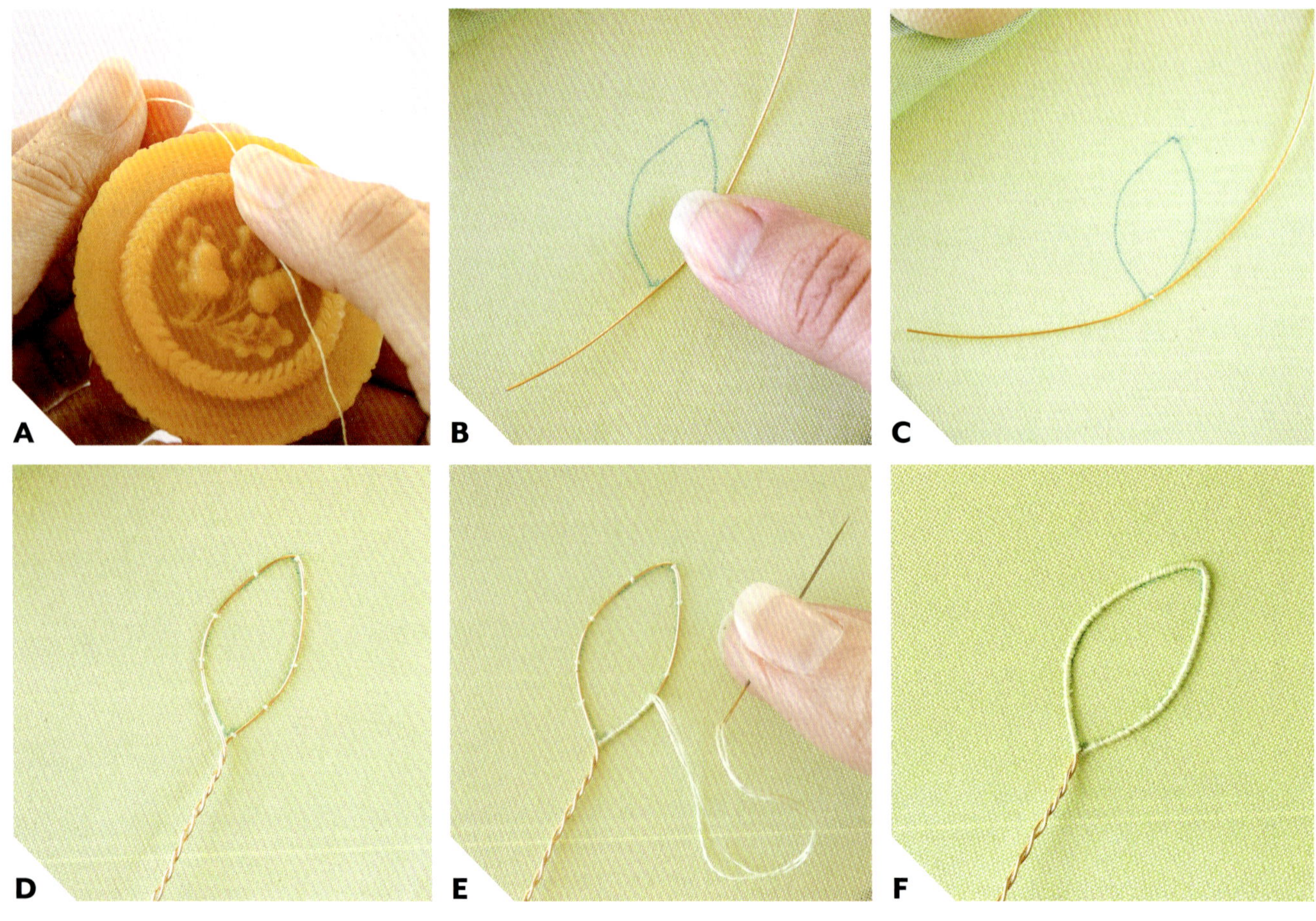

6. Embroider the interior of the wire slip. **G**

7. Cut the wire slip out of the fabric carefully with small, pointed scissors. Cut up to but not into the stitches. **H**

8. Paint the edges of the wire slip with fabric glue and a fine-tipped paint brush. **I**

9. Using a tapestry needle, create a hole on the fabric base where you want to attach the wire slip. **J**

10. Insert the wire ends into the hole. **K**

11. Couch stitch through the base of the wire slip with a matching thread color to secure it. The wire slip can stand freely now; bend or shape as desired. **L-M**

Fabric Techniques

Padded Applique

Padded applique is an easy and effective way to incorporate unique and striking three-dimensional textures into an embroidery design. I recommend exploring specialty fabrics, such as embossed and printed vinyl fabrics, faux fur, and textured felts for this technique. These fabrics are well suited for applique because the cut edges will not fray (see Fabric, page 11). For this tutorial, I am using a faux-grass fabric with felt backing that is typically used for crafting but suitable for applique as well.

1. Couch stitch around the edge of the applique fabric to attach it to the base fabric. Space stitches close together, approximately 5mm apart. **A**

• THREAD COLOR •

Select a thread that matches the fabric even though it will be hidden in the high pile of this fabric. Alternatively, use a transparent thread, such as Sulky Invisible Thread.

2. Leave a small section of the appliqued fabric unstitched. **B**

3. Stuff wool roving or polyester filling into the opening until filled and firm. **C**

4. Couch stitch the opening closed. **D**

A

B

C

D

A long, pronged stuffing tool, such as the Benzie Design stuffing tool, is a helpful device for filling applique designs with roving or other filling.

Silk Botanicals

This is an extremely versatile technique for adding three-dimensional fabric elements to a design. This tutorial models how to create leaves from silk fabric, though the same method can be applied to other fabrics and designs. Pre-treating the fabric with a fabric stiffener is essential to the technique. It prevents the fabric from fraying and creates a canvas that can be altered by drawing mediums and shaped by folding and heat. The fabric becomes more paper-like and can be treated as such. See Materials (page 10) for more information about recommended fabric stiffeners and dying mediums.

1. Soak the fabric in the fabric stiffener for 1–2 minutes, until thoroughly saturated. **A**

> **• FABRIC STIFFENER STRENGTH •**
>
> *You can dilute fabric stiffener with water to create a more flexible hold. I recommend using 2 tablespoons of Mod Podge Plaid Stiffy Fabric Stiffener for every 1 tablespoon of water. This mixture will yield a more realistic leaf texture, pliable yet firm. Alternatively, undiluted Jacquard Fabric Sculpting Medium will yield a stiff, more permanent hold that mimics sculpture made of harder material.*

2. Lay the fabric onto wax paper to dry. Smooth out any bubbles or wrinkles. **B**

3. Paint or dye the dried fabric using your preferred method or as directed by the project instructions. I use Jacquard Green Label Silk Dyes and a watercolor brush to paint my fabric. Lay flat to dry. **C**

4. Trace the design onto the fabric with a white fabric chalk pencil or other erasable transfer method. Use sharp, pointed scissors to cut out the designs. **D**

5. Use a mini-iron to press details like folds, wrinkles, or textures into the design. **E-F**

> **• SILK FLORAL TOOLS •**
>
> *A Clover Mini Iron is a versatile and widely accessible tool for pressing details into silk florals. The spade-shaped tip is suitable for most details. A regular clothing iron can be used as a substitute to the mini iron; just be mindful when ironing on small designs and use only the tip or edge of the larger iron to avoid injury. If you want to explore more specialty tools with a wide range of precise tips for various sculpting results, I highly recommend Steven Cooper Metalsmith's brass forming tools.*

A

B

C

D

E

Ironing in leaf veins

F

Beads

Wrapped Beads

Transform plain wooden beads by wrapping them with thread or ribbon. This technique is commonly used to create round botanical elements, such as flower buds or berries.

1. Thread a sharp, long chenille needle with embroidery thread. Leave the thread unknotted. Bring the thread through the bead and leave a 1½˝ (3.8cm) tail hanging from the end. I used 3 strands of 6-stranded embroidery floss for this tutorial. It's up to you how many strands and what kind of fiber to use. **A**

2. Bring the needle back through the bead from the same direction as in Step 1. **B**

3. Pull taut to create a loop around the bead. **C**

4. Repeat Steps 2–3 to create a second loop next to the first. Gently push the threaded loops together to remove any gap. Repeat until the bead is covered. **D**

5. Carefully trim away the thread ends. **E**

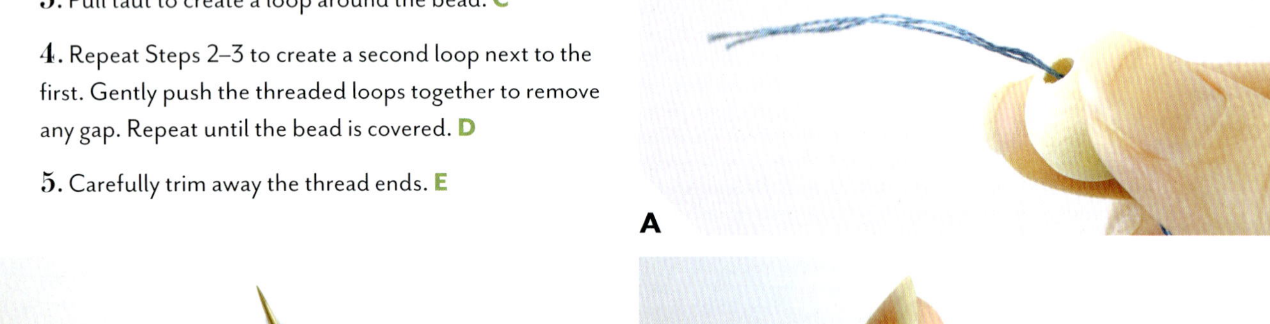

A

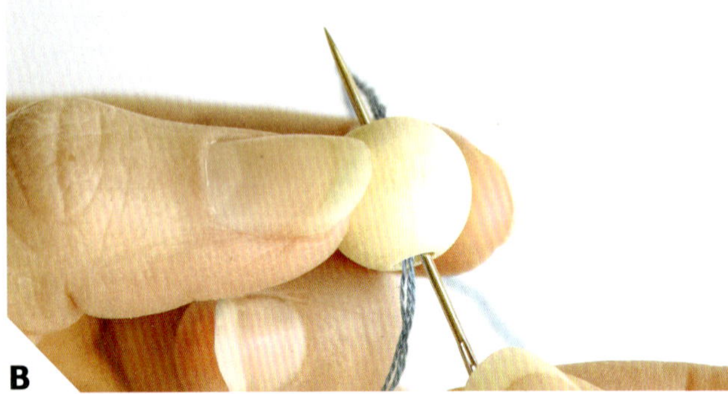

B

C

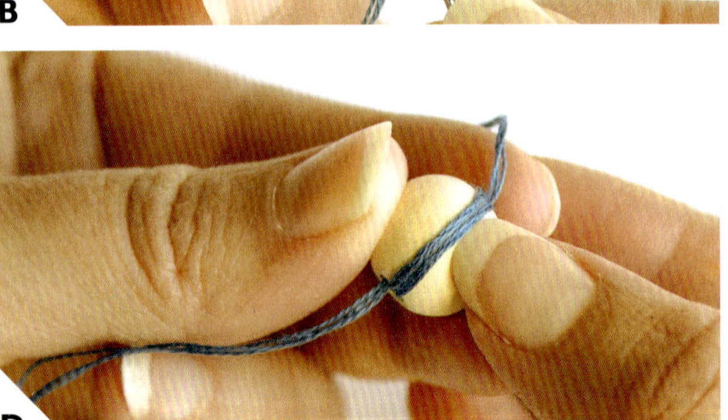

D

E

Beaded Slips

Beaded slips can be used to create round clusters of beads. This technique is useful for making three-dimensional botanical elements, such as berries or pollen-dotted flower centers. This model demonstrates a beaded slip with size #8 seed beads. Feel free to experiment with different types and sizes of beads for a different look. Or, substitute the beads altogether for French knots to create a fully embroidered version. The background fabric and thread colors should closely match the bead color for a cohesive look.

1. Thread a beading needle with sewing thread, Sulky invisible thread, or 1 strand of cotton embroidery floss that matches the bead color.

2. Begin at the top of the shape. Bring the needle up and through the bead. Bring the needle back down next to the beginning point, attaching it to the fabric. **A**

3. Secure the bead with a second pass of the needle through the bead and fabric. The extra stitch ensures the beads remain anchored through the assembly stage. **B**

4. Repeat Steps 2–3 to create rows of beads side-by-side until the shape is filled. **C**

5. Cut around the beaded slip with a ⅝" (1.6cm) margin. Use a size 9 embroidery needle and 1 strand of cotton embroidery thread to make a running stitch around the beaded slip. Leave the extra thread attached and do not tie off the end. **D**

6. Place a pinch of wool roving or polyester filling on the backside of the beaded slip. **E**

7. Pull the excess thread to tighten the running stitch around the wool and cinch the fabric together around the filling. **F**

8. Stitch the thread back and forth across the backside of the slip, catching the excess fabric with each pass of the needle and maintaining tension, until the slip is securely closed. **G-H**

Minimize gaps by stitching the beads close together in uniform rows.

Matching color of roving

FAUNA

Forest Mother of Pearl Butterfly

FINISHED PROJECT SIZE: 2¼˝ × 2½˝ (5.7 × 6.4cm)

The mother of pearl butterfly has a remarkably unique and otherworldly appearance. True to its name, this butterfly's wings have a pearlescent glow and appear to transform in color depending on the angle and light. This color-shifting phenomenon is due to the microscopic scales of its wings which refract light at different angles. To recreate an illusion of this beautiful effect, this project blends a pearlescent filament through the thread-painted wings. Be sure to display your finished embroidery near a light source to fully appreciate the shimmer and shine.

Materials

5¼˝ (13.3cm) embroidery hoop

Size 8 and 10 embroidery needles

Tapestry needle

Thread conditioner

24 gauge jewelry wire

Wire cutters

Small, pointed scissors

Fabric glue

Craft-quality detail paint brush

Benzie Design Corriedale wool roving: Smoke Grey

38 Gauge Cross Star felting needle

Needle felting pad

Graphite tracing paper (black and white)

Forest Mother of Pearl Wings pattern (page 156)

Forest Mother of Pearl Body pattern (page 156)

Frame or display hoop, optional

Thread and Fabric

7˝ (17.8cm) square of KONA cotton in Foxglove

2 squares 8˝ × 8˝ (20.3 × 20.3cm) of KONA cotton in Eggplant

1 spool of COSMO Nishikiito Metallic Thread #101 (Glass)

1 skein each of the following DMC 6-stranded cotton embroidery floss colors

STITCHES USED IN THIS PROJECT

Couch Stitch, page 30

Long and Short Stitch, page 31

Back Stitch, page 26

Straight Stitch, page 25

Satin Stitch, page 28

Transfer the Pattern

See Transferring Patterns (page 23) for more information.

> **• WIRE POSITION •**
> *Position the wing pattern so that the ends of the wire slips will face outward. This helps keep the wires out the way when you are embroidering the wings.*

1. Transfer the Forest Mother of Pearl Wings pattern onto the square of KONA Foxglove using your preferred method. I used black graphite paper. Secure in the 5¼″ (13.3cm) embroidery hoop. **A**

2. Transfer the Forest Mother of Pearl Body pattern centered onto the square of KONA Eggplant using your preferred method. I used white graphite paper. **B**

Prepare the Wire Slips

See Wire Slips (page 38) for more information about creating wire slips. Couch the wire slips with 1 strand of DMC cotton embroidery floss and a size 10 needle.

1. Prepare thread with thread conditioner. Couch stitch the 24 gauge jewelry wire around the forewings with DMC 09 and 762. Twist the wire ends together. **C**

2. Couch stitch the 24 gauge jewelry wire around the hindwings with DMC 09 and 762. Twist the wire ends together. **D-E**

> **• WIRES •**
> *Curve the wire ends around the edge of the hoop or tape them down so they sit flat against the fabric and do not snag the thread.*

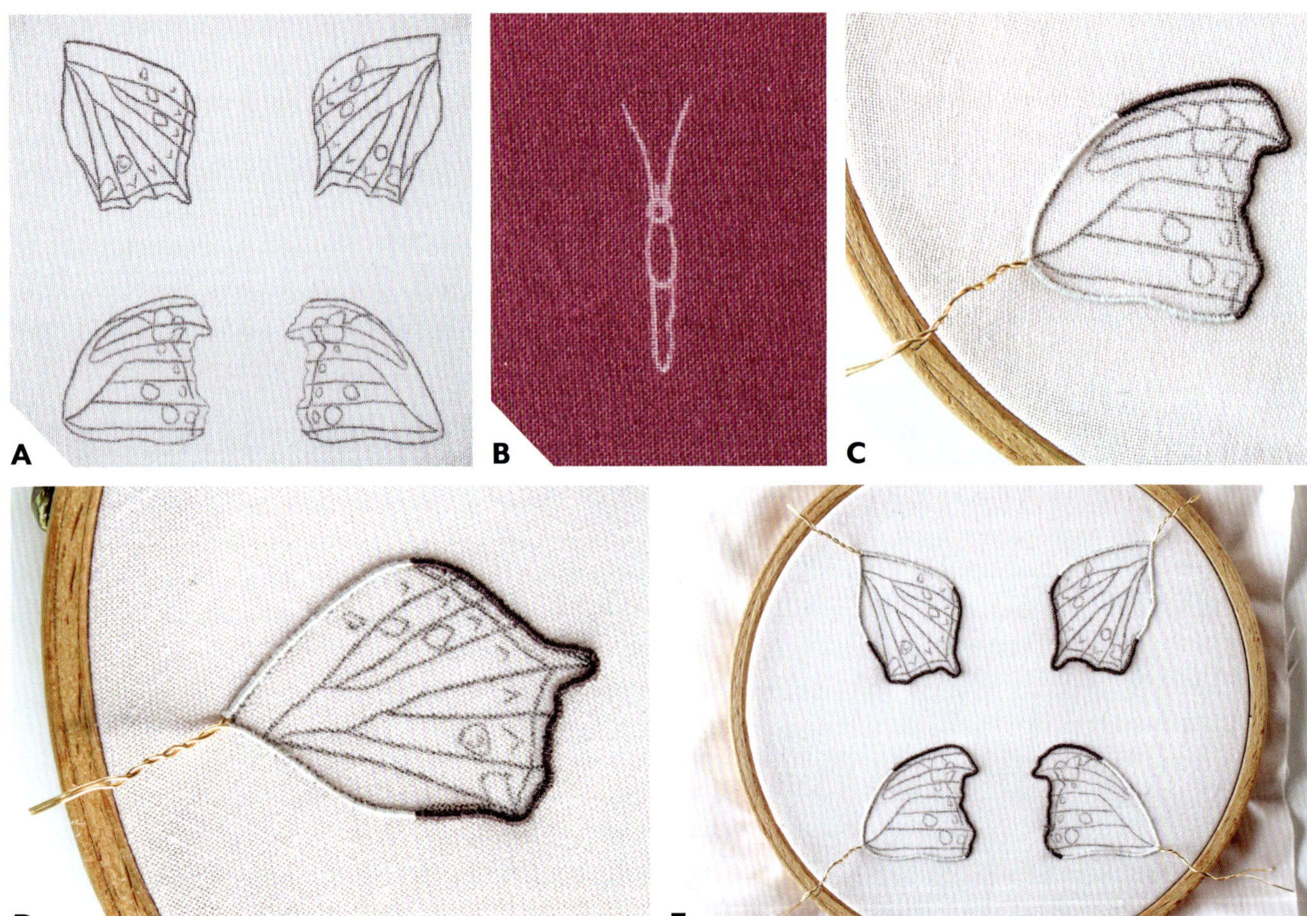

Embroider the Forewings

Stitch the forewings with 1 strand of DMC embroidery floss and a size 10 embroidery needle unless otherwise specified. The stitch direction starts at the inner corner and follows the curve of the wing. When creating the slight gradient within each wing section, stitch the darker colors closer to the inner corner of the wing.

1. Fill the outer edge of the wing with long and short stitches of DMC 09. Satin stitch the spots with 09. **A**

2. Blend DMC 24, 25, and 26 with long and short stitches to fill the wing. Leave narrow gaps for the wing veins. **B**

3. Backstitch the wing veins with DMC 452. **C**

4. With a size 8 needle, blend straight stitches of COSMO Nishikiito 101 (Glass) throughout each section of the wing for a pearlescent effect. **D**

5. Repeat Steps 1–4 with the other forewing.

· WORKING WITH METALLIC THREADS ·

When embroidering with metallic threads, keep the working thread length 8˝ (20.3cm) or shorter and use a size 8 or larger needle. Metallic threads are prone to tangling and fraying when passed through the fabric repeatedly, so a larger needle and shorter thread length reduces repeated friction. Thread conditioner can also help make metallic threads more manageable.

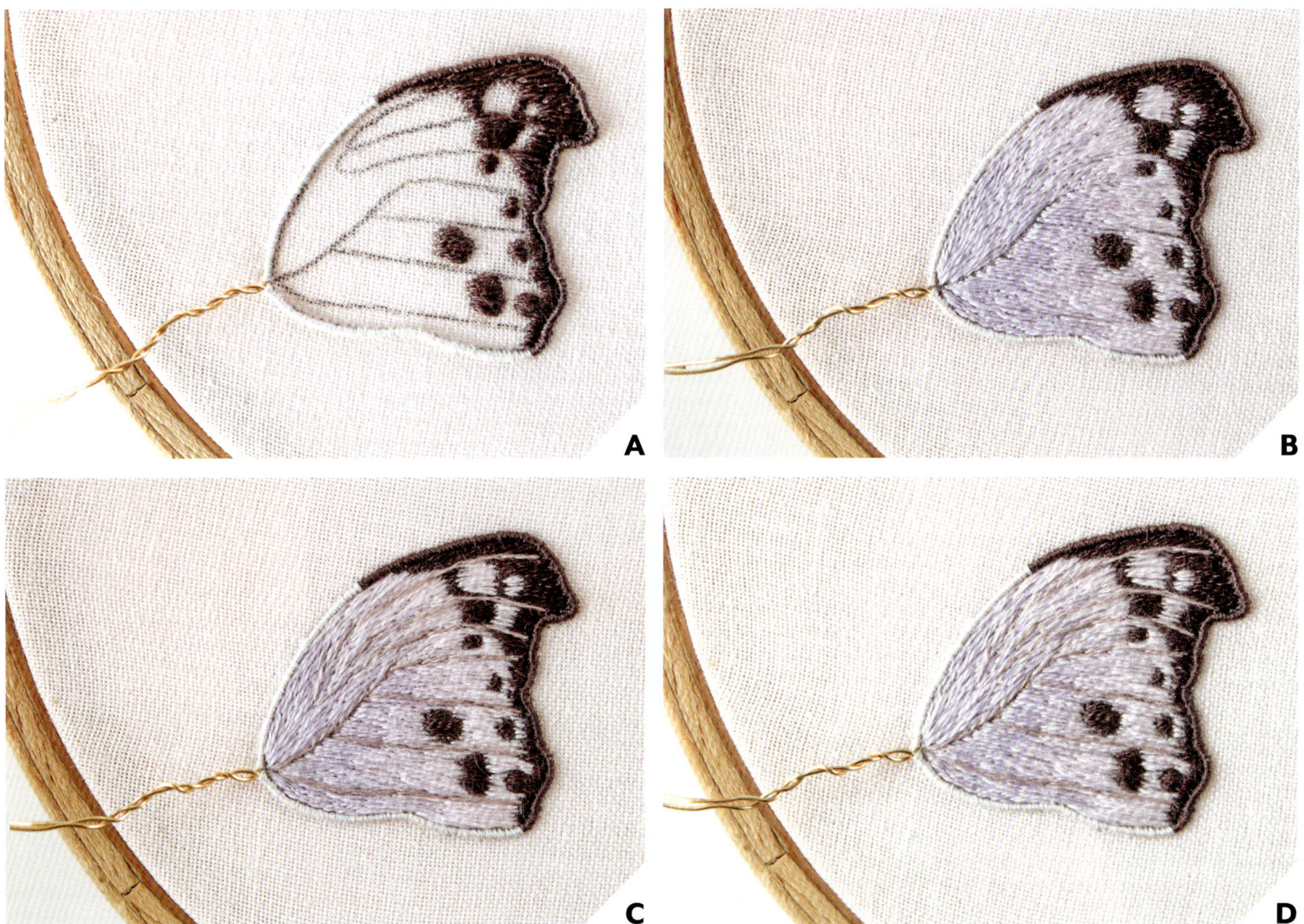

Embroider the Hindwings

Stitch the hindwings with 1 strand of DMC embroidery floss and a size 10 embroidery needle unless otherwise specified. The stitch direction starts at the inner corner and follows the curve of the wing.

1. Fill the outer edge of the wing with long and short stitches of DMC 09. Satin stitch the spots with DMC 09. **A**

2. Blend DMC 24, 25, and 26 with long and short stitches to fill the wing. Leave narrow gaps for the wing veins. **B**

3. Satin stitch the eye spot with rings of DMC 17, 24, and 34. Outline the eye spot with backstitches of DMC 09. **C**

4. Backstitch the veins with DMC 452. **D**

5. With a size 8 needle, blend straight stitches of COSMO Nishikiito 101 (Glass) throughout each section of the wing for a pearlescent effect. **E**

6. Repeat Steps 1–5 for the other hindwing. Remove the fabric from the hoop. **F**

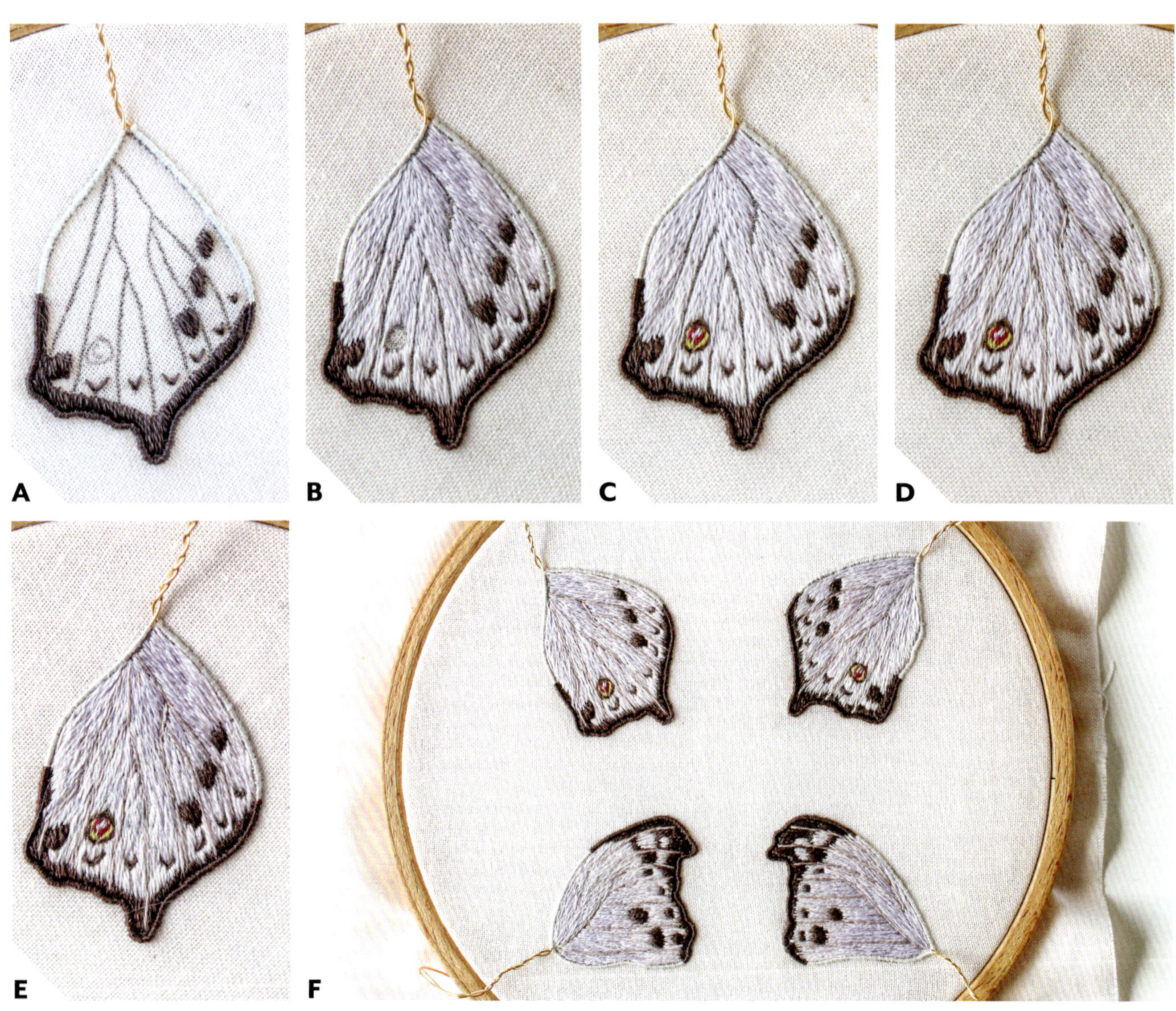

A B C D E F

Prepare the Padded Base

See Needle-Felted Padding (page 34) for more information on felted padding.

1. Layer both pieces of KONA Eggplant in the 5¼˝ (13.3cm) hoop with the pattern on top.

2. Felt the Corriedale wool roving with the 38 gauge star-tipped felting needle to fill the shape of the body. Trim any flyaway fibers to create a smooth padded base. Stagger the height of the felt so the head and abdomen are raised higher than the torso. **A**

Embroider the Body

Stitch the body with 1 strand of DMC embroidery floss and a size 10 embroidery needle.

1. Satin stitch the head and torso in 2 sections with DMC 04. Satin stitch the lower abdomen with DMC 03. Backstitch the antennae with DMC 413. **B**

Assembly

See Wire Slips (page 38) for more information about cutting out, gluing, and attaching the wings to the body.

1. Cut away all excess fabric from the wings. Carefully apply fabric glue to the backs and edges of the wings. Let the wings dry completely. **C**

2. Refer to the pattern and mark the 4 spots where the wings attach to the body with a pencil or air-soluble marker. Use the tapestry needle to make a hole in each spot. Attach the wings to the body by guiding the wire through the holes. Couch stitch the wings in place with DMC 762 at the inner corner of each wing. **D**

3. See Displaying Embroidery (page 16) for instructions on how to secure your butterfly in a hoop or in a frame. I transferred mine to a floral mosaic frame with matching colors.

Old World Swallowtail Butterfly

FINISHED PROJECT SIZE: 5˝ × 3˝ (12.7 × 7.6cm)

Butterflies are one of my favorite subjects to embroider, and for good reason. These small and beautiful creatures serve such an important role as pollinators and harbingers of spring. Their vibrant colors signal the shift from pale winter greys to the bright displays of spring florals. Swallowtail butterflies in particular are admired for their bold colors and unique wing shape. This project combines thread painting with padding and wire stumpwork techniques to create a realistic butterfly that looks ready to fly out of the hoop.

Materials

6½˝ (16.5cm) embroidery hoop

Size 10 embroidery needle

Tapestry needle

Thread conditioner

24 gauge jewelry wire

24 gauge paper-coated floral wire

Wire cutters

Small, pointed scissors

Fabric glue

Craft-quality detail paint brush

Benzie Design Corriedale wool roving: Latte, Black

38 Gauge Cross Star felting needle

Needle felting pad

Graphite transfer paper for tracing (white)

Old World Swallowtail Wings pattern (page 155)

Old World Swallowtail Body pattern (page 155)

Frame or display hoop (optional)

Thread and Fabric

2 squares 9˝ × 9˝ (22.9 × 22.9cm) of KONA cotton in Basil

10˝ × 10˝ (25.4 × 25.4cm) square of KONA cotton in Pepper

1 skein each of the following DMC 6-stranded cotton embroidery floss colors

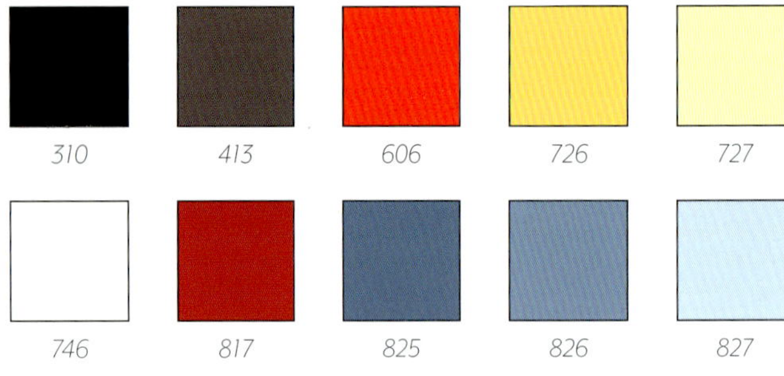

STITCHES USED IN THIS PROJECT

Couch Stitch, page 30

Back Stitch, page 26

Long and Short Stitch, page 31

Seed Stitch, page 25

Transfer the Pattern

See Transferring Patterns (page 23) for more information.

1. Transfer the Old World Swallowtail Wings pattern to the KONA Pepper fabric using your preferred method. I used white graphite transfer paper. Secure the fabric in the 6½″ (16.5cm) embroidery hoop. **A**

2. Transfer the Old World Swallowtail Body pattern to the center of the KONA Basil fabric using your preferred method. I used white graphite transfer paper. **B**

Prepare the Wire Slips

See Wire Slips (page 38) for more information about wire slips. Embroider the wire slips with a size 10 needle and 1 strand of DMC cotton embroidery floss.

1. Couch stitch the 24 gauge jewelry wire around the forewings with DMC 310 and 727. Twist the wire ends together. **C**

2. Couch stitch the 24 gauge jewelry wire around the hindwings with DMC 310, 727, and 746. Twist the wire ends together. **D**

3. Repeat Steps 1–2 until all four wire slips are couched. **E**

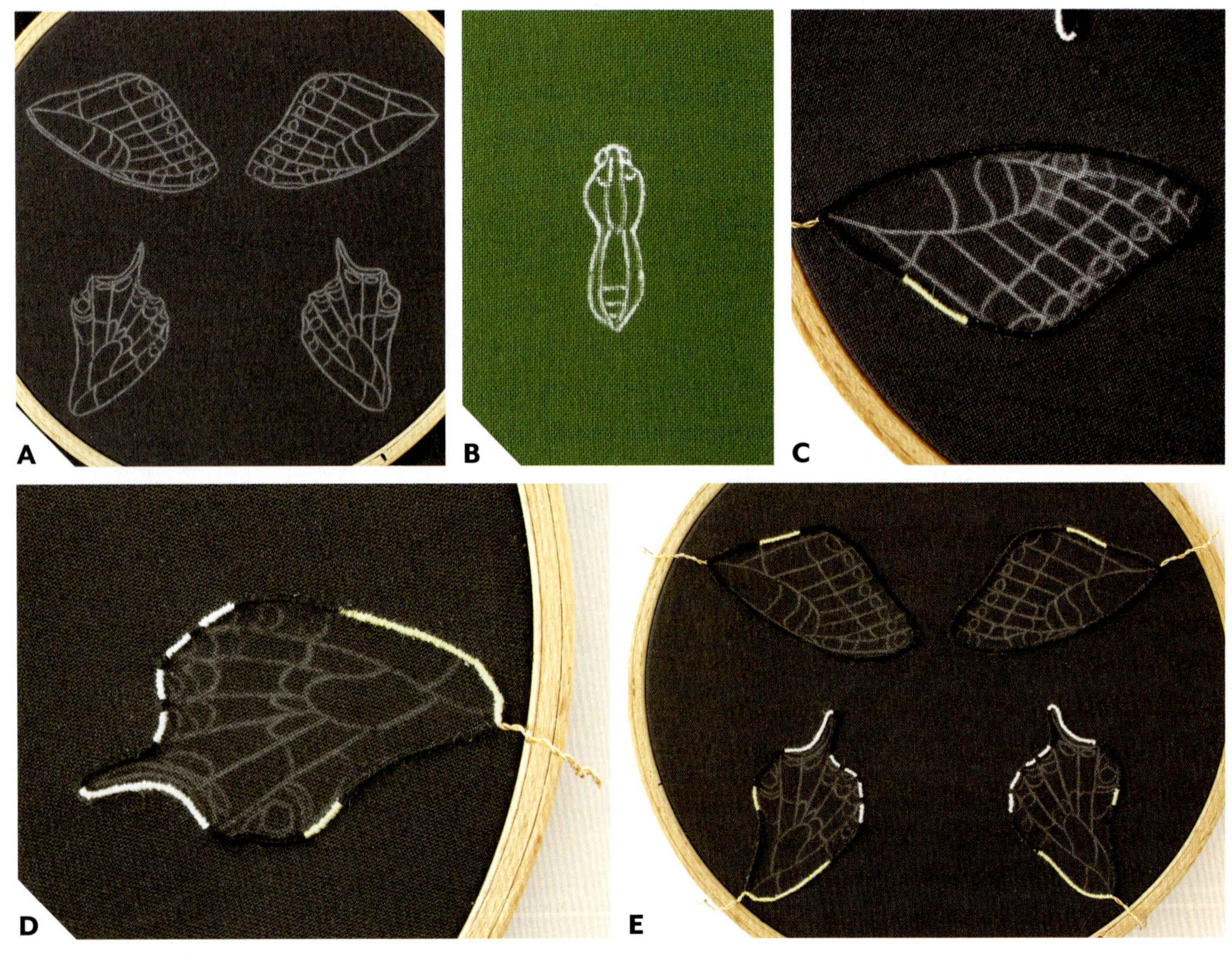

Embroider the Butterfly

Embroider the butterfly with 1 strand of DMC cotton embroidery thread and a size 10 embroidery needle unless otherwise specified.

Embroider the Forewings

1. Fill the sections on the edges of the forewing with long and short stitches of DMC 310 and 746. **A**

2. Blend long and short stitches of DMC 727 and 746 to fill the middle sections of the wing. **B**

3. Embroider tiny seed stitches of DMC 727 and 746 over the black areas of the wing. **C**

4. Backstitch the veins with DMC 413. **D**

5. Repeat Steps 1–4 with the other forewing.

Embroider the Hindwings

1. Fill the sections on the edges of the hindwing with long and short stitches of DMC 310 and 746. **E**

2. Blend long and short stitches of DMC 726 and 727 to fill the middle sections of the wing. **F**

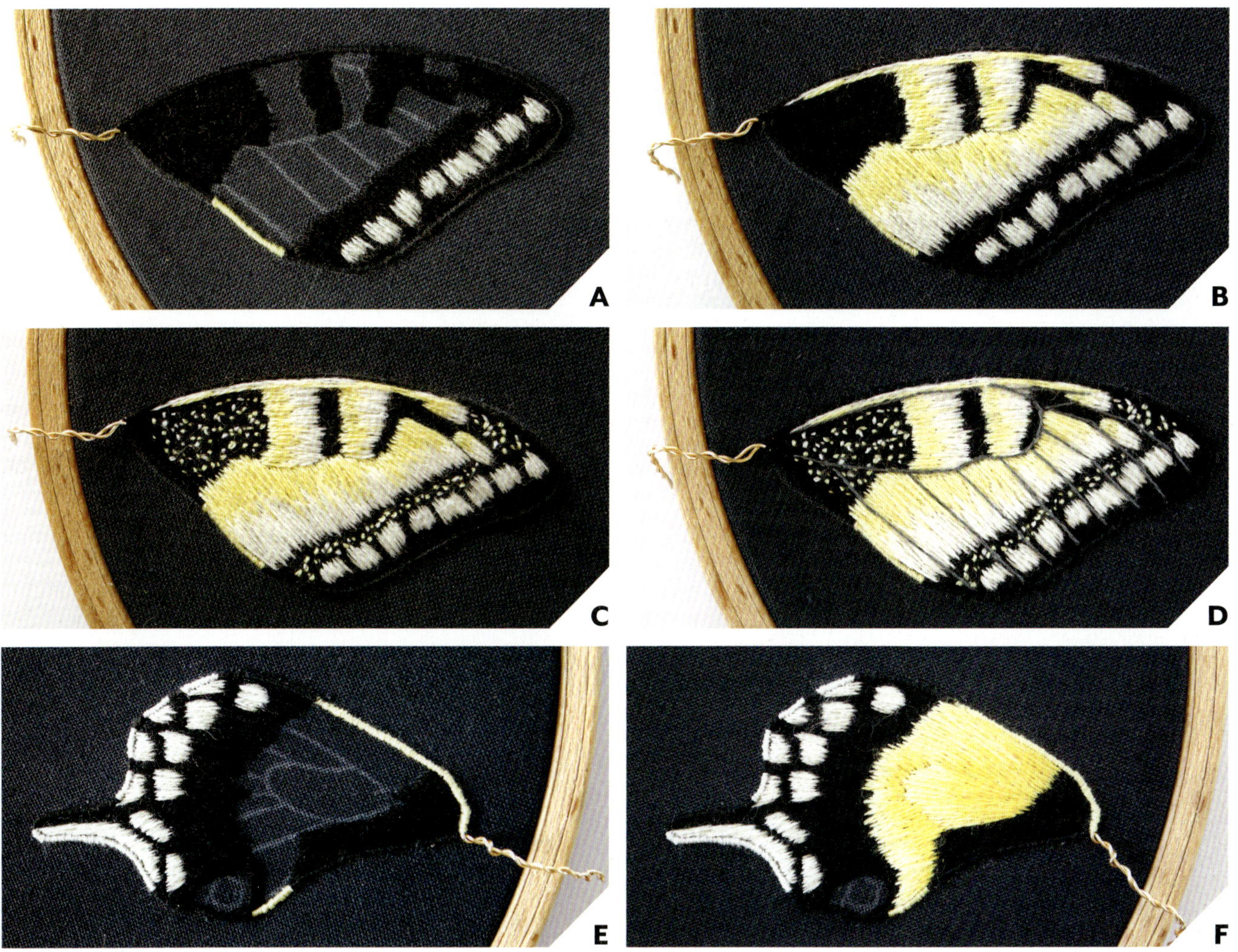

3. Embroider the eye spot with long and short stitches of DMC 826, 727, 606, and 817. G

4. Add small seed stitches of DMC 825, 826, 827, 727, and 746 over the black sections of the wing. H

5. Backstitch the veins with DMC 413. I

6. Repeat Steps 1–5 with the other hindwing. J

Prepare the Padded Base

See Padding (page 34) for more information.

1. Layer the 2 squares of KONA Basil fabric with the body pattern on top. Secure the layered fabric in the 6½˝ (16.5cm) hoop.

2. Felt the body with black and latte Corriedale wool roving and the 38 gauge felting needle until firm. Felt the center and head with black; fill the outer edges with latte. K

Embroider the Body

1. Embroider over the padded thorax with long and short stitches of DMC 310 (along the center) and DMC 727 (at the edges), covering the wool.

2. Add long and short stitches of DMC 746 to the middle section already embroidered with DMC 310. Overlap the stitches slightly to create a ruffled look. L

Embroider the Antennae

1. Cut 2 pieces of floral wire 1½˝ (3.8cm) long for the antennae. Wrap ⅝˝ (1.6cm) of each wire with 1 strand of DMC 310. See Wires (page 36) for more information. Set aside. M

Assembly

See Wire Slips (page 38) for more information about cutting out, gluing, and attaching the wings to the body.

1. Cut away all excess fabric from the wings. Carefully apply fabric glue to the backs and edges of the wings. Let the wings dry completely. **A**

A

2. Refer to the pattern and mark the 4 spots where the wings attach to the body with a pencil or air-soluble marker. Repeat for the antennae. Use the tapestry needle to make a hole in each spot. Attach the wings and antennae to the body by guiding the wire through the holes. Couch stitch the wings and antennae in place with DMC 310 at the inner corner of each wing and at the base of the antennae. **B**

B

3. See Displaying Embroidery (page 16) for instructions on how to secure your butterfly in a hoop or in a frame. I finished my butterfly in a hoop.

· FULLY 3-D BUTTERFLIES ·

To create a standalone butterfly, embroider the body on a piece of black fabric. When the embroidery is complete, closely cut around the body shape and secure the edges of the design with fabric glue. Cut a piece of black felt fabric to fit the backside of the body, and glue in place to cover the wires and stitching.

Swan

FINISHED PROJECT SIZE: 2½˝ × 4˝ (6.4 × 10.2cm)

Swans are admired for their unparalleled elegance and grace both in and out of the water. They are among my favorite birds to embroider. Rather than rely on white or grey thread colors, this swan is embroidered with an unexpected palette of aqua hues that complement the fabric color. The subtle shift in color values along the swan's features create more realistic shadows and an illusion of depth and perspective. The padded body also helps make the design pop against the fabric, while the watery details add movement and life to the design. Display your finished swan in a small frame for a dramatic break-the-frame effect.

Materials

5¼˝ (13.3cm) embroidery hoop

Size 8 and 10 embroidery needles

Tapestry needle

Size 10 beading needle

Thread conditioner

24 gauge jewelry wire

Wirecutters

Small, pointed scissors

Fabric glue

Craft-quality detail paint brush

Benzie Design Corriedale wool roving: White

38 Gauge Cross Star felting needle

Needle felting pad

Miyuki Rocailles transparent crystal beads size #11

Czech crystal glass transparent rainbow beads size #6

C&T Publishing Wash-Away Stitch Stabilizer paper

Graphite transfer paper (black)

Swan pattern (page 154)

Swan Wing pattern (page 154)

Frame or display hoop, optional

Fabric and Thread

8˝ × 8˝ (20.3 × 20.3cm) square of KONA cotton in White

2 squares 9˝ × 9˝ (22.9 × 22.9cm) of KONA cotton in Everglade

COSMO Nishikiito Metallic thread #101

1 skein each of the following DMC 6-stranded cotton embroidery floss colors

STITCHES USED IN THIS PROJECT

Couch Stitch, page 30

Satin Stitch, page 28

Long and Short Stitch, page 31

Peking Knot, page 28

French Knot, page 27

Seed Stitch, page 25

Transfer the Pattern

See Transferring Patterns (page 23) for more information.

1. Transfer the Swan Wing pattern to the 8˝ × 8˝ (20.3 × 20.3cm) square of KONA cotton in White. Secure the fabric in the 5¼˝ (13.3cm) embroidery hoop. **A**

2. Print or draw the Swan pattern onto the water-soluble stitch stabilizer paper. Follow the printing instructions on the package. Set aside the stickers for later.

Prepare the Wire Slip and Felted Wing

See Wire Slips (page 38) for more information about wire slips and Needle-Felted Padding (page 34) for more on felted padding.

1. Couch the 24 gauge jewelry wire around the wing with 1 strand of DMC BLANC and the size 10 embroidery needle. The wire ends do not meet in this design, so don't twist them together. There should be a gap of approximately ¼˝ (7mm) between the beginning and end of the wireslip. **B**

2. Use the 38 gauge star-tipped felting needle and white Corriedale wool roving to felt the three upper sections of the wing. Create a stepped look with the padding, shaping it to match the round pattern lines. The uppermost section should have the most height and padding. Gradually decrease the height of the padding with each remaining section. The lowest sections of the wing have no padding. **C**

Embroider the Wing

Embroider the wing with 1 strand of DMC cotton embroidery floss and a size 10 embroidery needle unless otherwise specified.

1. Embroider long and short stitches of DMC 964 to the underside of the first and second rows of feathers to define their scalloped edges. **D**

2. Blend long and short stitches of DMC 3756 and BLANC to fill the two middle sections of the wing with a subtle ombre effect (darker color at upper edge of each section). **E**

3. Embroider the top row of feathers with long and short stitches of DMC BLANC. **F**

4. Embroider the bottom row of feathers with long and short stitches of DMC 3756 and BLANC, again stitching the darker color at the upper edge of the section. **G**

A

B

I *Define the feathers by felting grooves into the padding.*

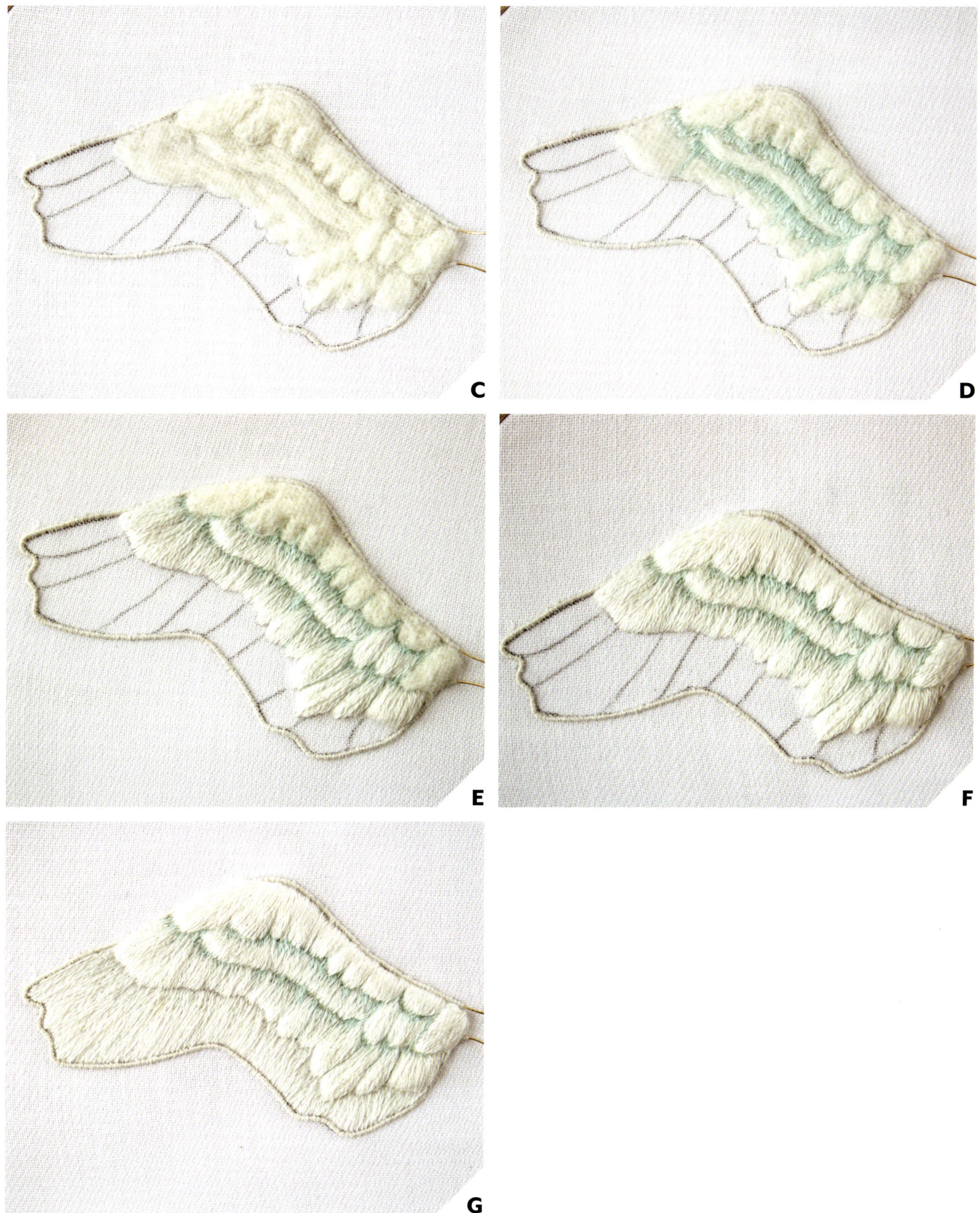

Prepare the Padded Base

See Padding (page 33) for more information about padded stumpwork.

1. Secure the 2 squares of KONA cotton Everglade in the 5¼″ (13.3cm) embroidery hoop.

2. Retrieve the Swan pattern stickers that were set aside earlier. Transfer the 2 body shape stickers to the sheet of wool felt. Cut out each shape. Remove the stickers so only the felt shapes remain. **A**

3. Thread a size 10 needle with 1 strand of DMC BLANC. Couch stitch the smaller felt shape onto the fabric. Couch stitch the second piece on top. **B**

4. Peel away the back of the Swan pattern sticker and adhere it to the base fabric, aligning the body with the padded felt outline. **C**

Embroider the Swan

Embroider the swan with 1 strand of DMC cotton embroidery floss and a size 10 embroidery needle unless otherwise specified.

Head

1. Satin stitch the eye mask with DMC 310. **D**

2. Fill the beak with long and short stitches of DMC 3854 and 720. **E**

3. Embroider the head with long and short stitches of DMC BLANC. Add long and short stitches of DMC 3756 and 964 along the underside of the chin and neck. Gently angle the stitches to follow the shape of the head. **F**

4. Embroider the neck with long and short stitches of DMC BLANC, 3756, 964, 3849, and 3848. **G**

Body

1. Fill the body with long and short stitches of DMC BLANC, 3756, 964, 3849, and 3848. Begin at the water line with DMC 3848 and gently curve the stitches toward the tail feathers to follow the rounded shape of the body. Blend the colors from dark to light as you move up the body. **H**

• STITCHING FEATHERS •

Your long and short stitches do not have to be perfectly and neatly blended. Allow some stitches to slightly overlap to create a more realistic, ruffled look to the feathers.

A

B

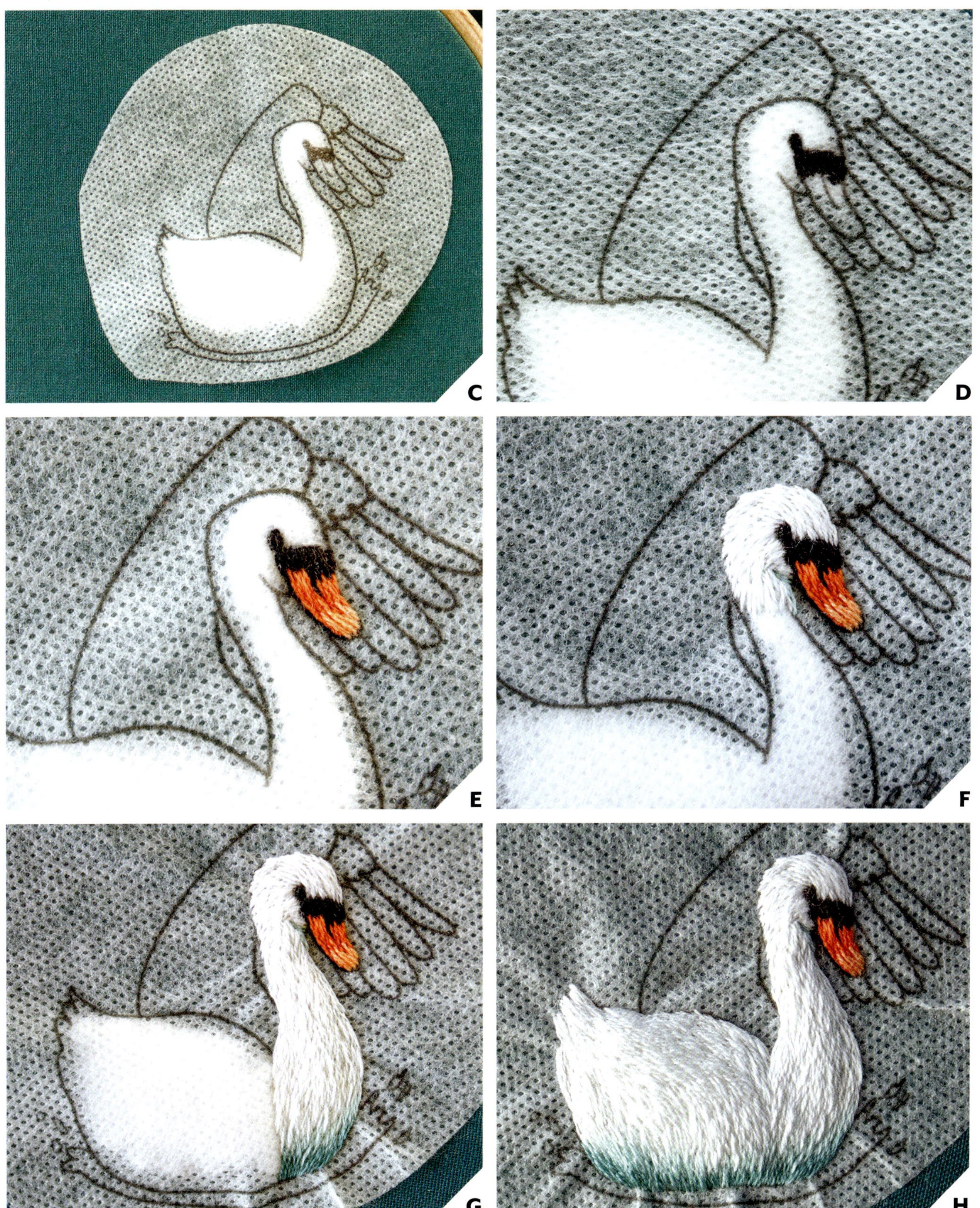
C
D
E
F
G
H

Back Wing

1. Begin at the area between the neck and body with the darkest colors. Fill the shoulder with long and short stitches of DMC BLANC, 3756, 964, 3849, and 3848. Angle the stitches outward to fill the wing shape. **A**

2. Embroider the feathers with long and short stitches of DMC BLANC, 3756, and 964. **B**

Embroider the Water

Embroider the water with 1 strand of DMC cotton embroidery floss and a size 10 embroidery needle unless otherwise specified.

Waterline

1. Embroider the water with long and short stitches of BLANC, 3756, and 964. **C**

2. Wash away the sticker transfer paper, and lay the fabric flat to dry. Secure the fabric back in the embroidery hoop once dry.

Bubbles

1. Thread a size 8 needle and 1 strand of DMC BLANC. Embroider a variety of seed stitches and French and Peking knots at the waterline. **D**

2. Repeat Step 1 with the Cosmo Nishikiito Metallic thread #101.

3. Thread the beading needle with 1 strand of DMC BLANC. Attach beads to the waterline at random.

Assembly

See Wire Slips (page 38) for more information about cutting out, gluing, and attaching the wing to the body.

1. Cut away all excess fabric from the wing. Carefully apply fabric glue to the backs and edges of the wing. Let dry completely. **E**

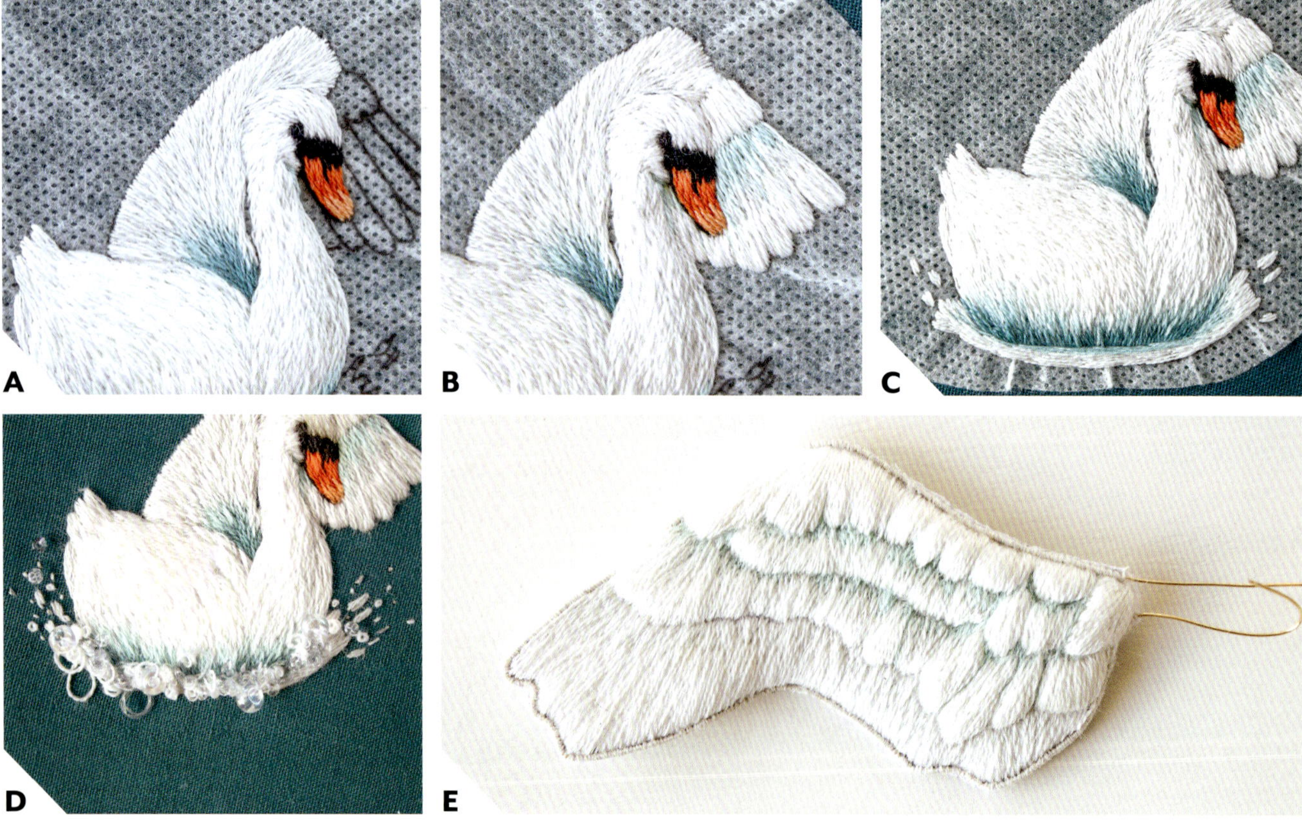

A B C D E

2. Refer to the pattern and mark the 2 spots where the wing attaches to the body with a pencil or air-soluble marker. Use the tapestry needle to make a hole in each spot. Attach the wing to the body by guiding the wires through the holes. Embroider long and short stitches of DMC BLANC that cross between the wing and the body to secure the wing in place and blend the feathers into the body. F

3. See Displaying Embroidery (page 16) for instructions on how to secure your swan in a hoop or in a frame. I displayed my finished swan in a vintage gilded frame.

F

Io Moth

FINISHED PROJECT SIZE: 4˝ × 2½˝ (10.2 × 5.1cm)

The Io moth, also known as a peacock moth, has two distinct colorways and wing patterns. While male Io moths are predominantly yellow, females display a beautiful array of autumnal colors with large, bold eye spots. This pattern combines needle felted padding, wrapped wires, wire slips, and thread painting to create a realistic female moth that appears ready to fly off into the night.

Materials

5¼˝ (13.3cm) embroidery hoop
Size 10, 8, and 7 embroidery needles
Tapestry needle
Thread conditioner
24 gauge jewelry wire
30 gauge paper-coated floral wire
Wire cutters
Small, pointed scissor
Fabric glue
Craft-quality detail paint brush
Benzie Design Corriedale wool roving: Oats, Orange
38 Gauge Cross Star felting needle
Needle felting pad
Graphite tracing paper (white and black)
Io Moth Wings pattern (page 150)
Io Moth Body pattern (page 150)
Frame or display hoop, optional

Thread and Fabric

8˝ × 8˝ (20.3 × 20.3cm) square of KONA cotton in Doeskin

2 squares 9˝ × 9˝ (22.9 × 22.9cm) of KONA cotton in Evergreen

1 skein each of the following DMC 6-strand embroidery floss colors

STITCHES USED IN THIS PROJECT

Couch Stitch, page 30
Straight Stitch, page 25
Long and Short Stitch, page 31
Turkey Stitch, page 29
Seed Stitch, page 25
Back Stitch, page 26

Transfer the Pattern

See Transferring Patterns (page 23) for more information.

1. Transfer the Io Moth Wings pattern onto the square of KONA Doeskin using your preferred method. I used black graphite paper. Secure in the 5¼″ (13.3cm) embroidery hoop. **A**

2. Transfer the Io Moth Body pattern onto the center of the square of KONA Evergreen using your preferred method. I used white graphite paper. **B**

Prepare the Wire Slips

See Wire Slips (page 38) for more information about creating wire slips. Couch the wire slips with 1 strand of DMC cotton embroidery floss and a size 10 needle. Prepare the thread with thread conditioner.

1. Couch stitch the 24 gauge jewelry wire around the forewings with DMC 919. Twist the wire ends together. **C**

2. Couch stitch the 24 gauge jewelry wire around the hindwings with DMC 353 and 06. Twist the wire ends together. **D-E**

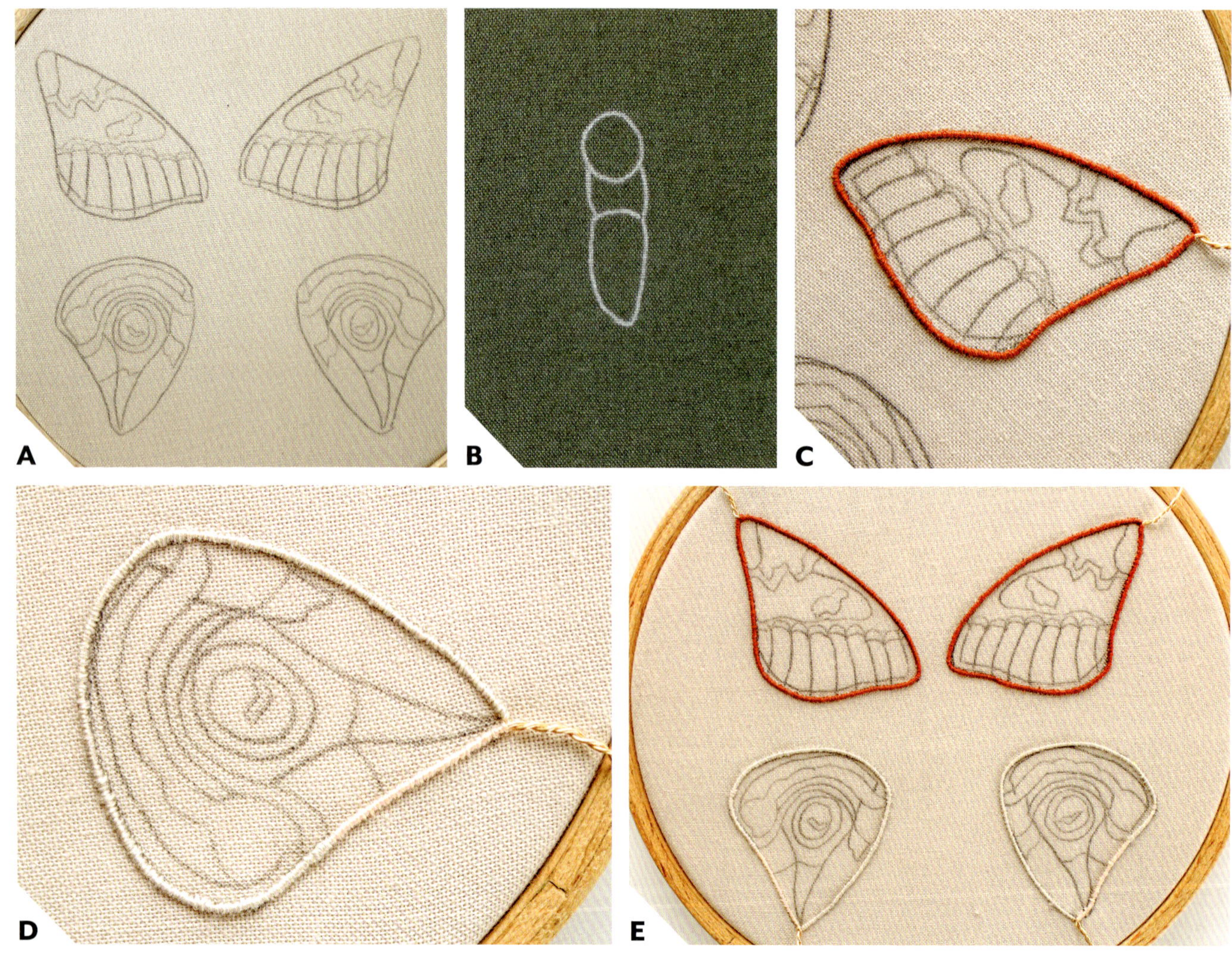

Embroider the Forewings

Stitch each wing with 1 strand of DMC embroidery floss and a size 10 embroidery needle unless otherwise specified. The stitch direction starts at the inner corner and follows the curve of the wing.

1. Embroider the inner corner of the wing with long and short stitches of DMC 918, 3865, and 06. **A**

2. Use 2 strands of DMC 4130 and a size 8 needle to fill the remaining section in the corner with turkey stitch. Trim the stitches to create a rounded shape and fluffy texture. **B**

3. Fill the midsections with long and short stitches of DMC 301, 3860, and 3865. **C**

4. Blend long and short stitches of DMC 3865, 3860, 3861, and 301 to fill the remaining part of the wing. **D**

5. Back stitch the wing veins with DMC 301. **E**

6. Repeat Steps 1–5 for the other forewing.

Embroider the Hindwings

Stitch each wing with 1 strand of DMC embroidery floss and a size 10 embroidery needle unless otherwise specified. The stitch direction starts at the inner corner and follows the curve of the wing.

1. Begin at the inner corner of the hindwing. Embroider long and short stitches of DMC 06, 841, 842, and 3778 to fill the innermost sections. **F**

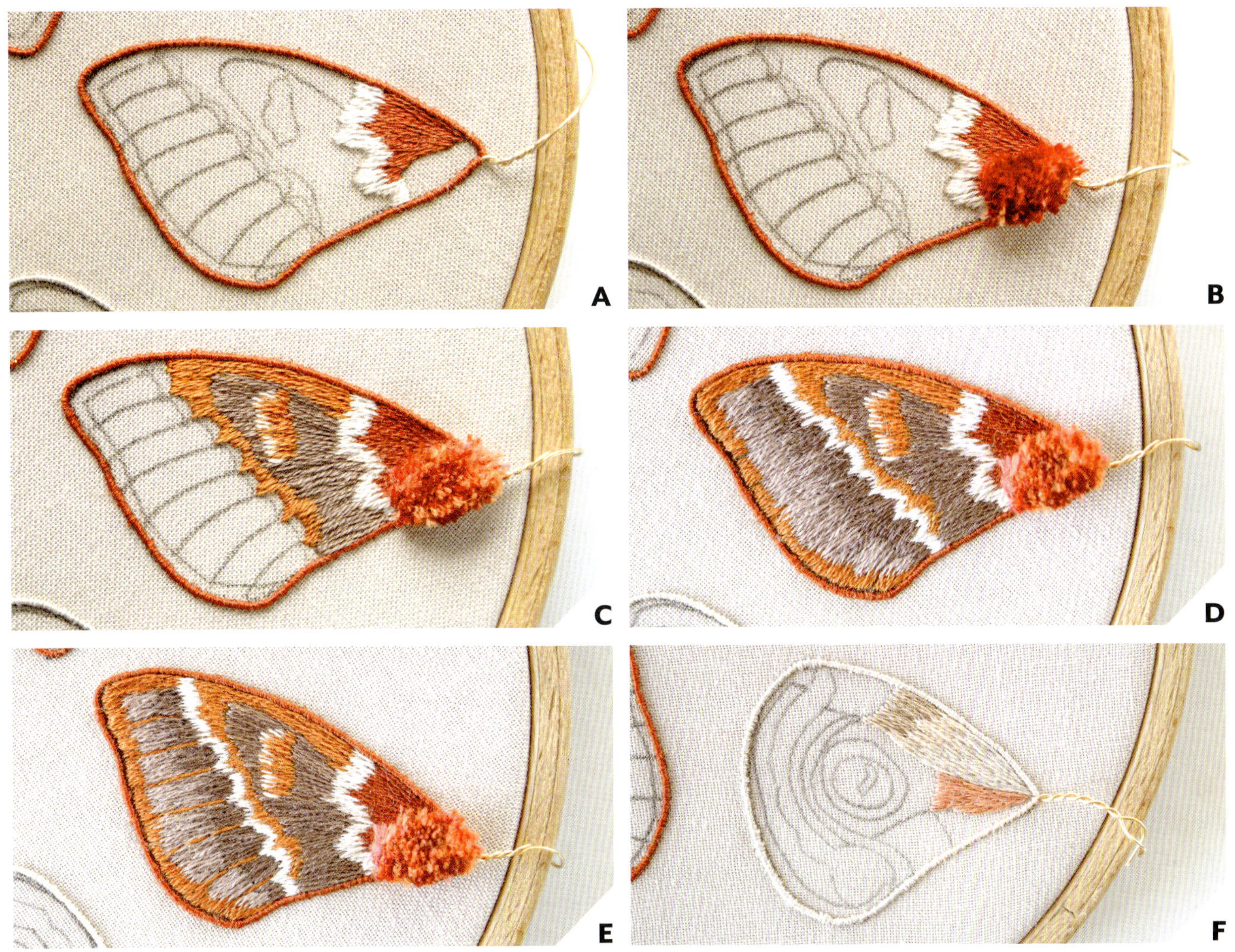

A B C D E F

2. Use 2 strands of DMC 351 and a size 8 needle to fill the remaining corner section with turkey stitch. Trim the stitches to create a rounded shape and fluffy texture. **G**

3. Blend long and short stitches of DMC 310 and 743 to fill the area around the eye spot. **H**

4. Fill the eye spot with long and short stitches of DMC 310, 04, and 3865. Add a few tiny seed stitches of DMC 310 and 3865 within the spot. **I**

5. Embroider the remaining three sections of the wing with long and short stitches of DMC 919, 3771, and 06. Blend each row of stitches into the row above it. **J**

6. Repeat Steps 1–5 with the other hindwing. **K**

Prepare the Padded Base

See Needle-Felted Padding (page 34) for more information on felted padding.

1. Layer both pieces of the KONA Evergreen fabric with the body pattern on top, and secure in the 5¼˝ (13.3cm) embroidery hoop.

2. Needle felt the thorax and abdomen with the 38 star felting needle and Corriedale wool. Create an orange rounded shape for the thorax and a cream oval for the abdomen. **L**

Embroider the Body

1. Use a size 10 needle and 1 strand of DMC 351 to embroider over and cover the padded abdomen with long and short stitches.

2. Make 5 horizontal straight stitches across the abdomen with 1 strand of DMC 3771. Space the stitches equally apart. **M**

3. Use a size 7 needle and 3 strands of DMC 4130 to cover the padded thorax with turkey stitch. Trim the stitches to create a rounded shape and fluffy texture. **N**

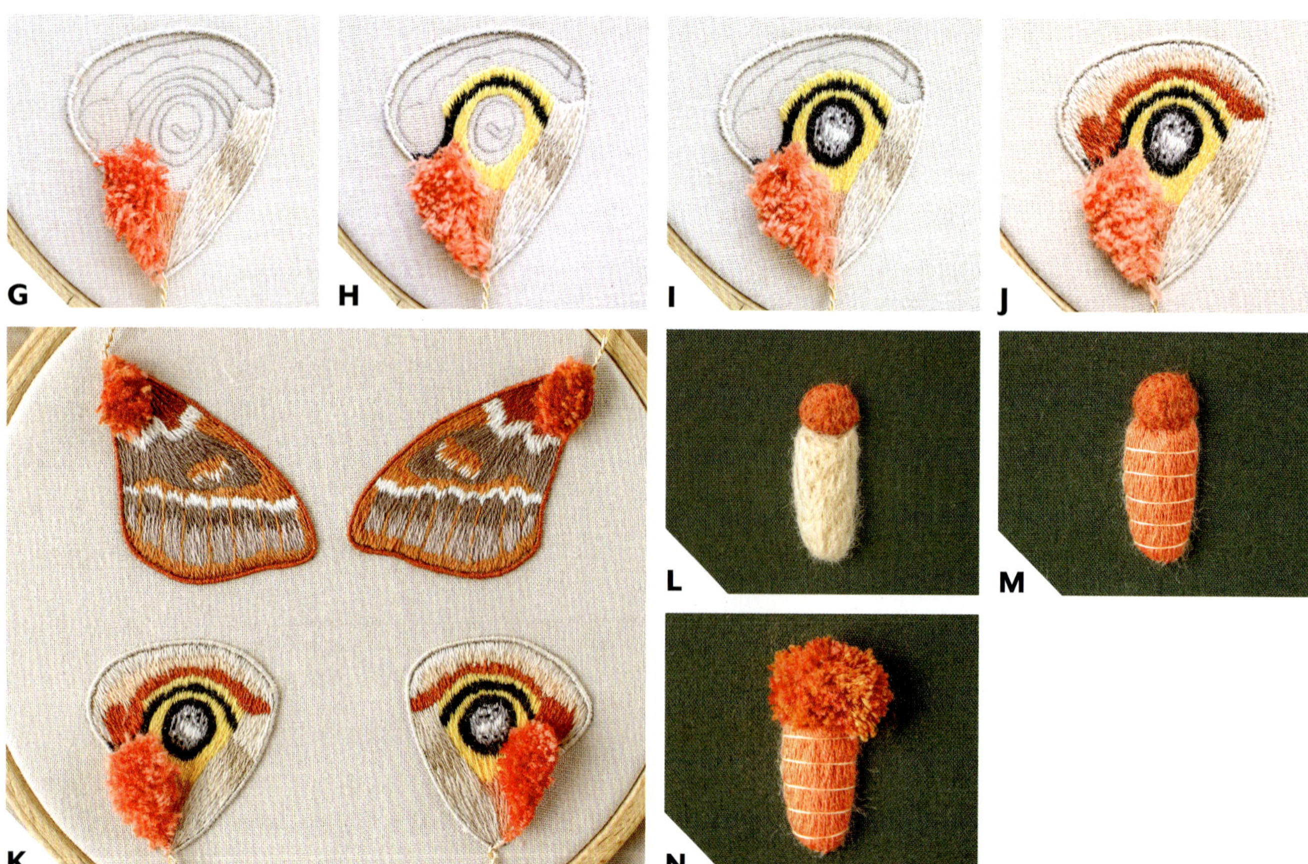

Make the Antennae

See Wires (page 36) for more information on thread-wrapped wires.

1. Cut two 1½˝ (3.8cm) pieces of 30 gauge floral wire. Wrap ¾˝ (1.9cm) of each wire with 1 strand of DMC 919. **A**

Assembly

See Wire Slips (page 38) for more information about cutting out, gluing, and attaching the wings to the body.

1. Cut away all excess fabric from the wings. Carefully apply fabric glue to the backs and edges of the wings. Let the wings dry completely. **B**

2. Use a tapestry needle to create 2 holes for the antennas at the top of the thorax. Insert the antennae into the holes and couch stitch in place with a size 10 embroidery needle and 1 strand of DMC 919.

3. Refer to the pattern and mark the 4 spots where the wings attach to the body with a pencil or air-soluble marker. Use the tapestry needle to make a hole in each spot. Attach the wings to the body by guiding the wire through the holes. Couch stitch the wings in place with DMC 4130 at the inner corner of each wing. **C**

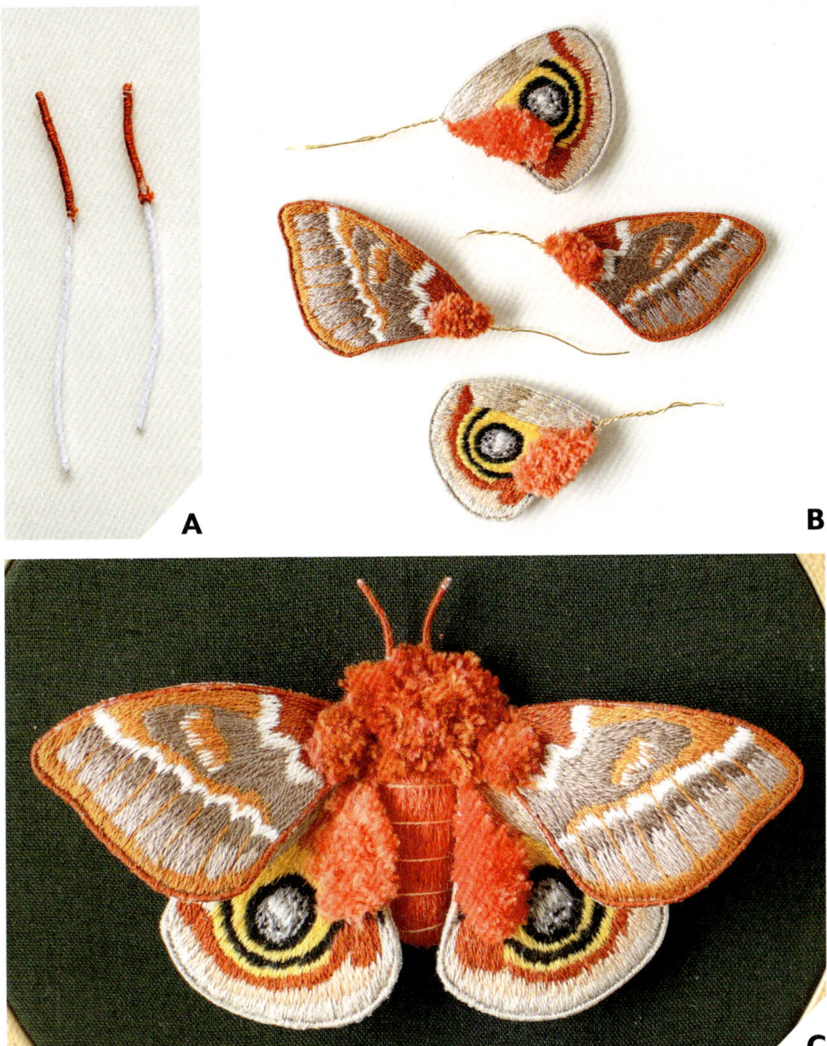

Finishing

See Displaying Embroidery (page 16) for instructions on how to secure your moth in a hoop or in a frame. I transferred my Io moth to a velvet green frame.

River Otter

FINISHED PROJECT SIZE: 4˝ × 5˝ (10.2 × 12.7cm)

River otters capture our collective adoration like no other animal! Their playful demeanor and impressive water aerobics make them such a fascinating animal to observe and embroider. This adorable otter is embroidered over layers of felt padding that make it subtly pop against the watery fabric. The painterly effect of the printed fabric adds an illusion of depth to this design, while the embroidered and beaded bubbles bring it to life with animated detail.

Materials

8˝ (20.3cm) embroidery hoop

Size 10 embroidery needle

Size 10 beading needle

Scissors

6/0 Czech clear iridescent glass beads

11/0 Miyuki Rocailles clear glass beads

C&T Publishing Wash-Away Stitch Stabilizer paper

River Otter pattern (page 153)

Frame or display hoop, optional

Fabric and Thread

2 squares 11˝ × 11˝ (27.9 × 27.9cm) of Sky Ombre by Jennifer Sampou for Robert Kaufman in Ocean

9˝ × 12˝ (22.9 × 30.5cm) sheet of Benzie Design wool felt in Latte

1 skein each of the following DMC 6-stranded cotton embroidery floss colors

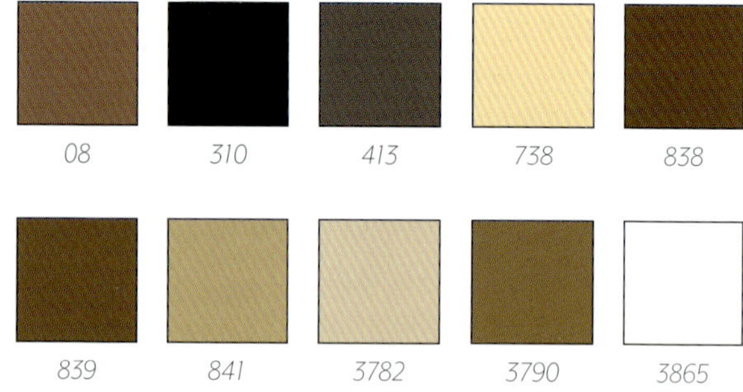

STITCHES USED IN THIS PROJECT

Couch Stitch, page 30

Satin Stitch, page 28

Long and Short Stitch, page 31

Peking Knot, page 28

French Knot, page 27

Seed Stitch, page 25

Straight Stitch, page 25

Transfer the Pattern

See Transferring Patterns (page 23) for more information.

1. Print or draw the River Otter pattern onto the Wash-Away Stitch Stabilizer paper. Follow the printing instructions on the package.

2. Cut out the padding body shape pieces from the sticker transfer paper. Leave a ¼˝ (6mm) margin around each shape. Attach the stickers to the sheet of wool felt. Set the remaining River Otter Pattern sticker aside until Step 5 of Prepare the Padded Base (right). **A**

3. Cut out each body shape from the wool felt without margins. Remove the stickers so only the felt shapes remain. Keep track of the numbered shapes. **B**

Prepare the Padded Base

See Padding (page 33) for more information.

1. Layer the pieces of Sky Ombre fabric. Secure both layers in the 8˝ (20.3cm) hoop and tighten the hardware until the fabric is drum-tight.

2. Thread a size 10 needle with one strand of DMC 738. Couch stitch the felt body outline #1 to the Sky Ombre fabric. **C**

3. Layer the felt body outline #2 over outline #1. Couch stitch the piece in place. **D**

4. Layer the felt body outline #3 over the other layers. Couch stitch the piece in place. **E**

5. Peel away the back of the River Otter pattern sticker and adhere it to the base fabric. Align the pattern with the padded felt outline. **F**

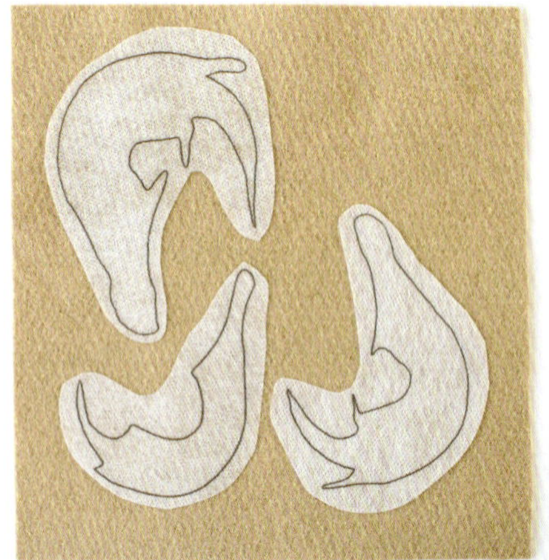

A

B

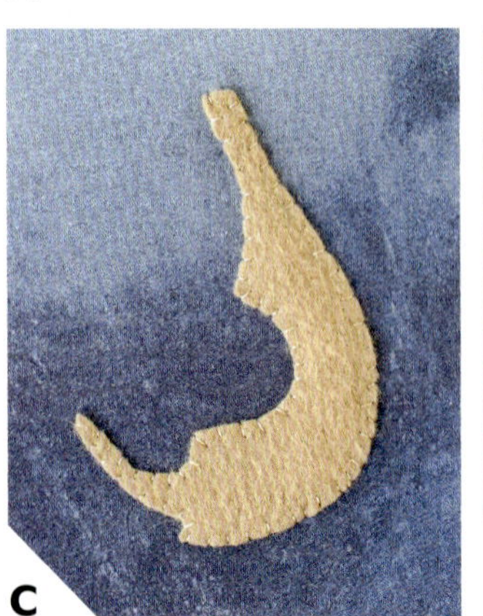

C

D

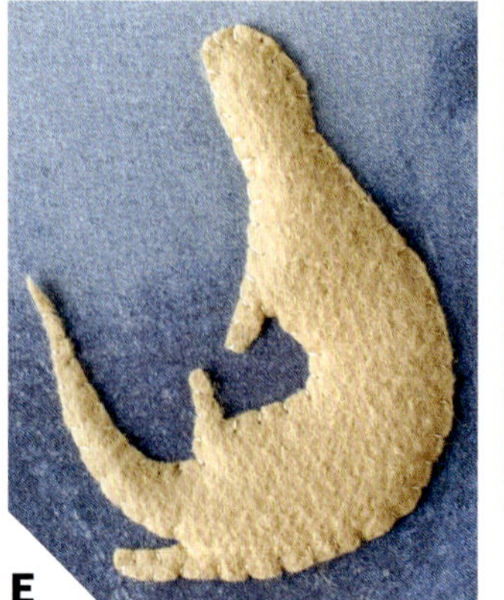

E

F

Embroider the Otter

Stitch with 1 strand of DMC 738 embroidery floss and a size 10 embroidery needle unless otherwise specified.

Face

1. Satin stitch the eye with DMC 310. Add a reflection at the top of the eye with seed stitches of DMC 3865 over the satin stitches of DMC 310. **A**

2. Satin stitch the nose with horizontal stitches of DMC 413. Fill in the muzzle with long and short stitches of DMC 3782. **B**

Chest

1. Embroider long and short stitches of DMC 841 from the muzzle down through the center of the chest. Blend random long and short stitches of DMC 3782 throughout the filled area of DMC 841. **C**

Ear

1. Fill the top of the head with long and short stitches of DMC 08.

2. Satin stitch the inner ear with DMC 839. Outline the shape of the ear with straight stitches of DMC 3782. Fill in long and short stitches of DMC 3782 and 841 to blend the ear with the cheek. **D**

· EMBROIDERING CURVED SHAPES ·

When embroidering a curved design such as this otter's ear, create a smoother and more natural looking shape by shortening the length of your stitches as you approach the top of the curve.

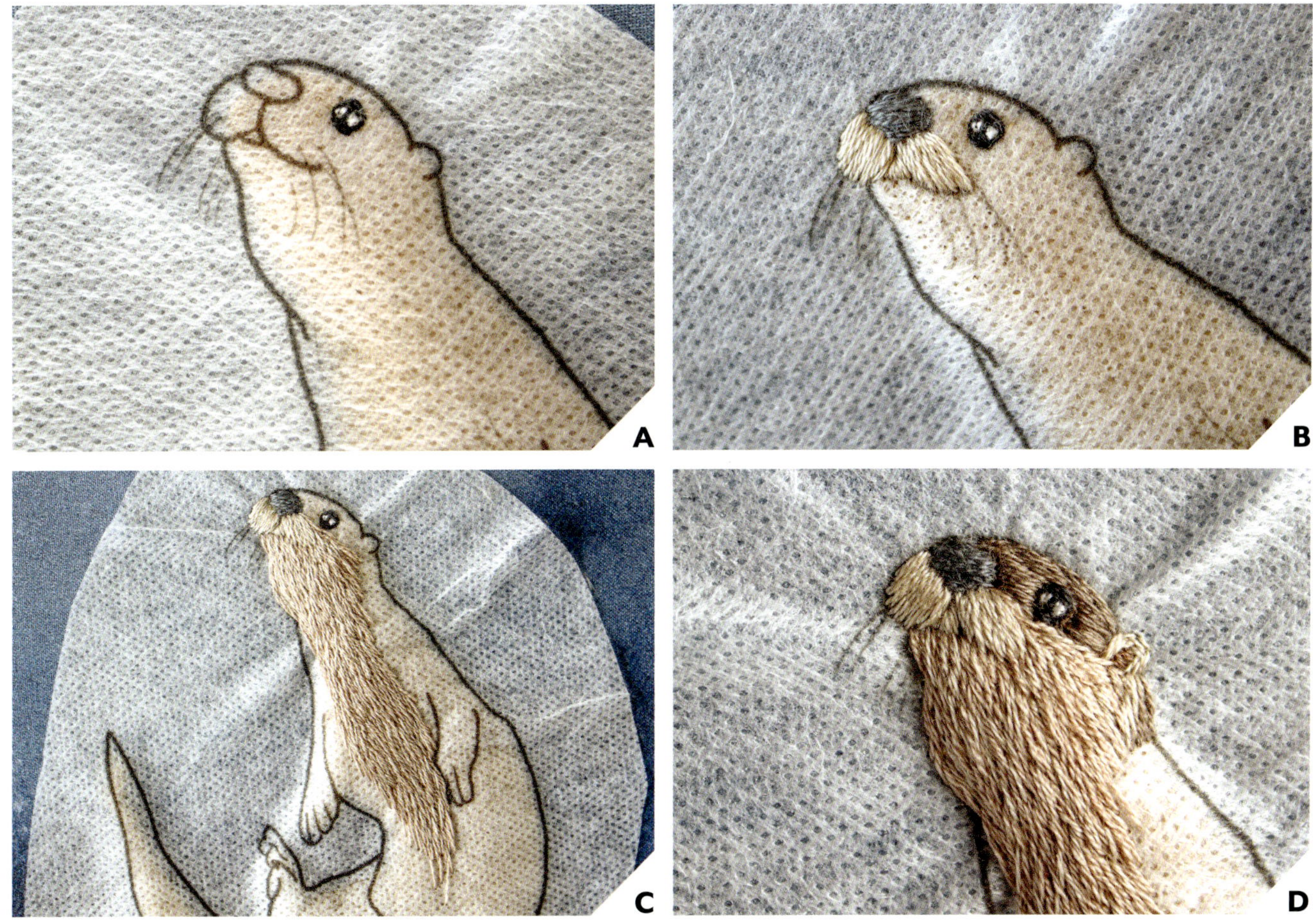

Arms & Torso

1. Fill in the arms with long and short stitches of DMC 08. Outline the shoulders, fingers, and arms with straight stitches of DMC 838. **A**

2. Fill in the torso with long and short stitches of DMC 3790, 08, and 839. **B**

Legs

1. Fill the legs with long and short stitches of DMC 08. Outline the toes and inner leg creases with straight stitches of DMC 838. **C**

Tail

1. Fill in the tail with long and short stitches of DMC 08 and 839. **D**

2. Wash away the stabilizer paper and lay flat to dry. Once dry, secure the embroidery back in the hoop.

Finishing Details

Embroider all finishing details with a size 10 embroidery needle and 1 strand of DMC 3865.

1. Embroider straight stitches angled downward on the cheeks to create whiskers. Add two small seed stitches to the nose as a highlight. **E**

2. Add five tiny seed stitches to each of the three paws that extend out into the water. **F**

Bubbles

1. Create bubbles around the otter with Peking knots, French knots, and seed stitches. Vary the size of the stitches to create a mix of small and large bubbles.

2. Attach 6/0 Czech clear iridescent glass beads and 11/0 Miyuki Rocailles clear glass beads throughout the embroidered bubbles with the size 10 beading needle and 1 strand of DMC 3865 to add extra texture and sparkle. **G**

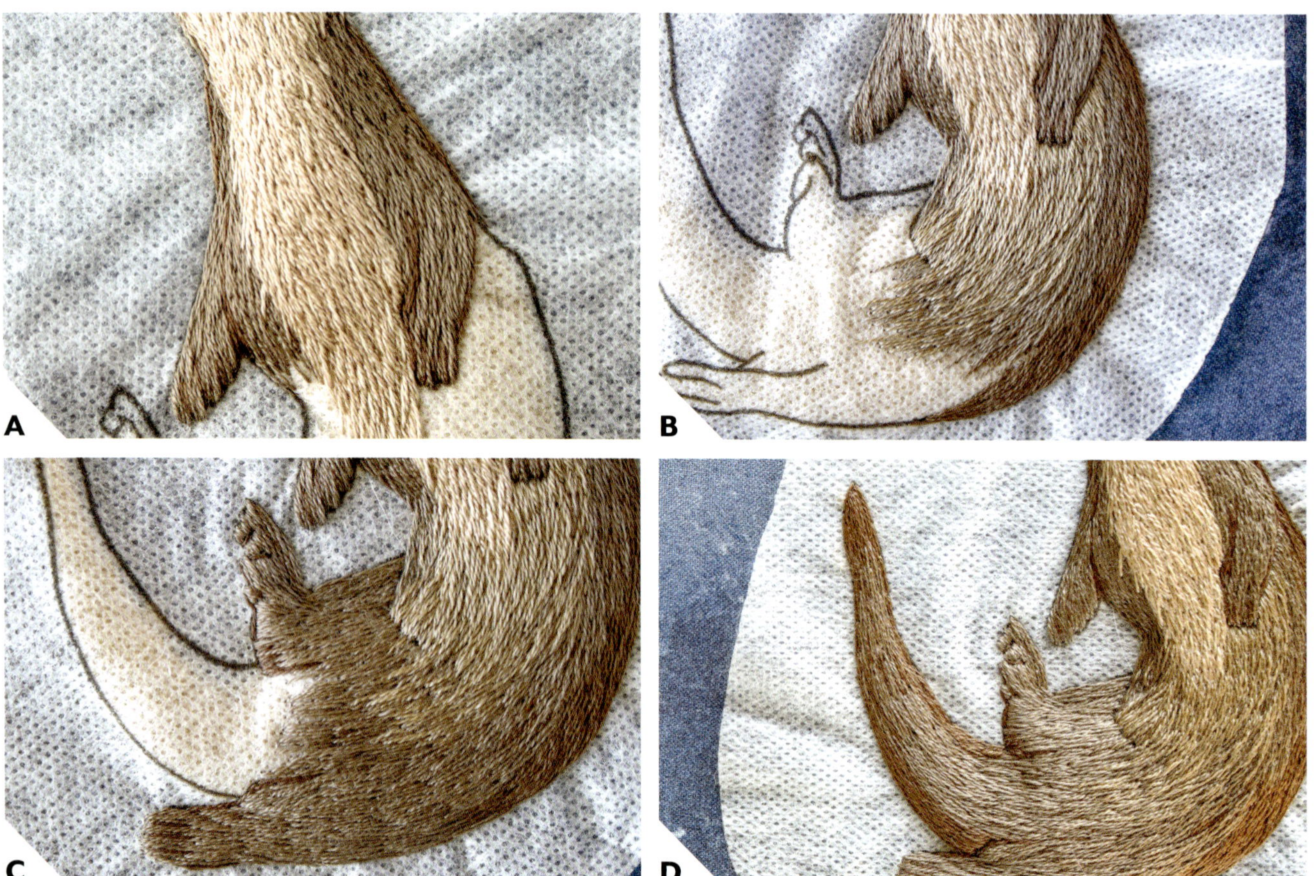

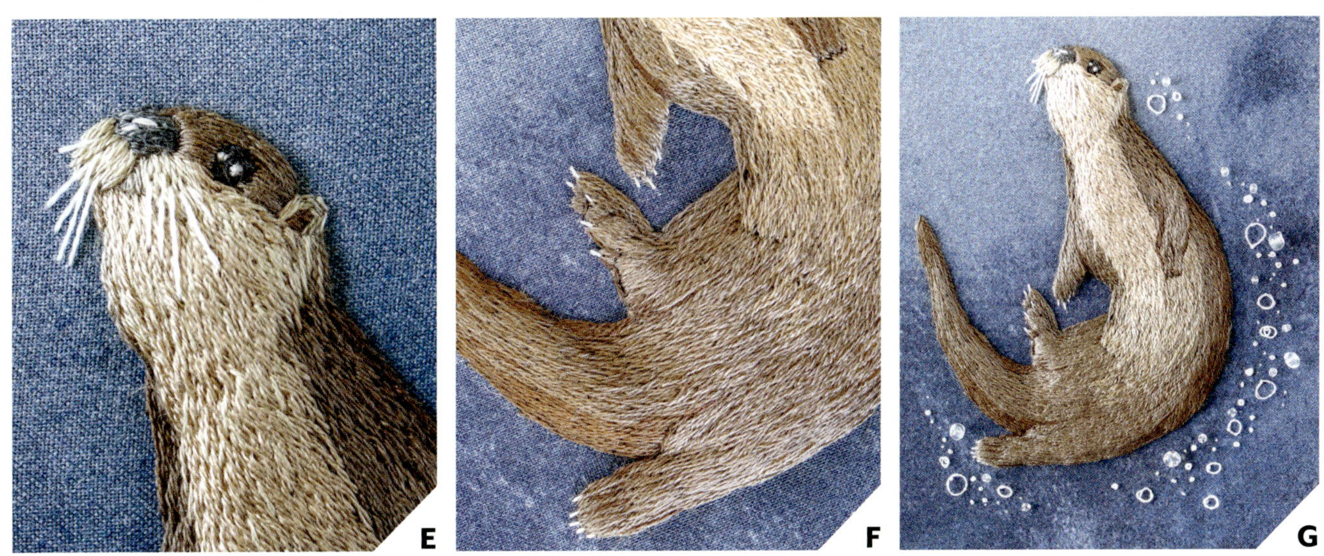

Finishing

See Displaying Embroidery (page 16) for instructions on how to secure your otter in a hoop or frame. I transferred mine to a Nurge display hoop.

Praying Mantis

FINISHED PROJECT SIZE: 3˝ × 4˝ (7.6 × 10.2cm)

When my children were very young, we had the unique opportunity to watch an ootheca (a praying mantis egg) hatch. Nearly two hundred tiny mantids poured out from the small, papery egg (much to my horror and my children's delight). Years later, we still occasionally spot the multi-generational offspring of our original mantids patrolling the garden beds. The memorable experience has made me a little less fearful of this intimidating-looking creature. In fact, it has become one of my favorite insects to embroider. Consider displaying your wire-slip and padded mantid in a rectangular frame or elongated oval to complement the insect's long, slender shape.

Materials

- 5¼˝ (13.3cm) and 6˝ (15.2cm) embroidery hoops
- Size 10 embroidery needle
- Tapestry needle
- Thread conditioner
- 24 gauge jewelry wire
- Wirecutters
- Small, pointed scissors
- Fabric glue
- Craft-quality detail paint brush
- Benzie Design Corriedale wool roving: Chartreuse, Oats
- 38 Gauge Cross Star felting needle
- Needle felting pad
- C&T Publishing Wash-Away Stitch Stabilizer paper
- Graphite transfer paper (white)
- Praying Mantis Body pattern (page 157)
- Praying Mantis Wings pattern (page 157)
- Frame or display hoop, optional

Fabric and Thread

- 7˝ × 7˝ (17.8 × 17.8cm) square of silk organza in White
- 2 squares 9˝ × 9˝ (22.9 × 22.9cm) of KONA Everglade
- 1 skein each of the following DMC 6-stranded cotton embroidery floss colors

STITCHES USED IN THIS PROJECT

- Couch Stitch, page 30
- Satin Stitch, page 28
- Long and Short Stitch, page 31
- Straight Stitch, page 25
- Split Stitch, page 26
- Back Stitch, page 26

Transfer the Pattern

See Transferring Patterns (page 23) for more information. Please note that you will transfer the Praying Mantis Body pattern twice for this project: once with sticker paper and once with graphite transfer paper.

1. Print or draw the Praying Mantis Body and Praying Mantis Wings patterns onto the Wash-Away Stitch Stabilizer paper. Follow the printing instructions on the package. Set aside the Praying Mantis Body sticker for later.

2. Secure the silk organza in the 6˝ (15.2cm) embroidery hoop. Peel away the back of the Praying Mantis Wing stickers and adhere them to the fabric. **A**

· HANDLING DELICATE FABRICS ·

Organza is more delicate than cotton or linen fabric. Use a light hand when securing the silk organza in the hoop to avoid tearing or distorting the weave of the fabric.

3. Transfer the Praying Mantis Body pattern to the KONA Everglade fabric using your preferred method. I used white graphite transfer paper. Do not use the body sticker pattern prepared in Step 1. **B**

Prepare the Wire Slips

See Wire Slips (page 38) for more information about wire slips. Couch the wire slips with 1 strand of DMC cotton embroidery floss and a size 10 needle.

1. Couch stitch the forewing wire slips with DMC 564. Twist the wire ends together. **C**

2. Couch stitch the hindwing wire slips with DMC 369. Twist the wire ends together. **D**

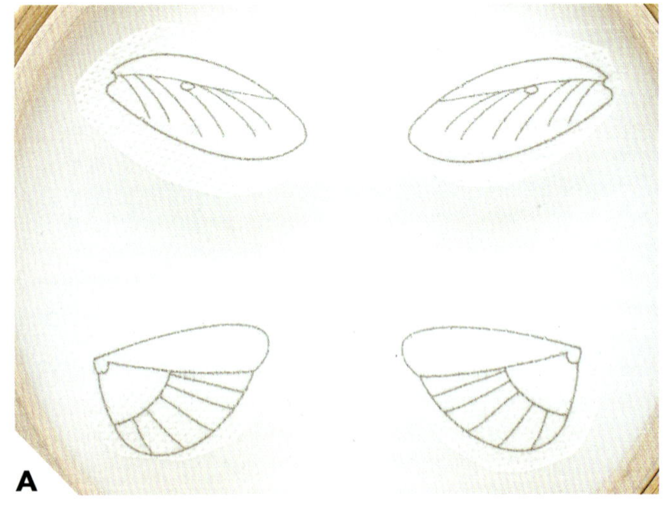

A

B

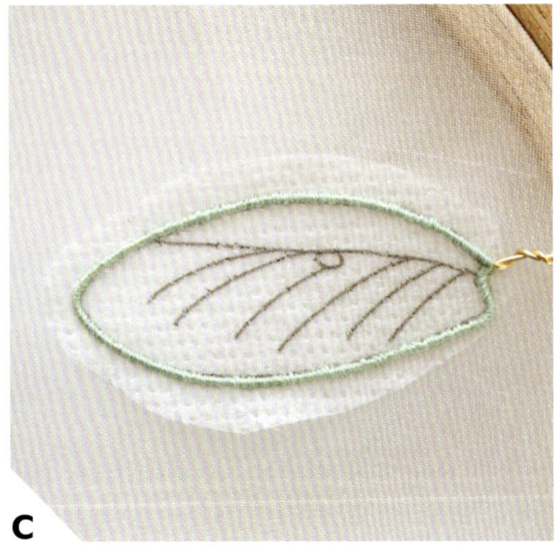

C

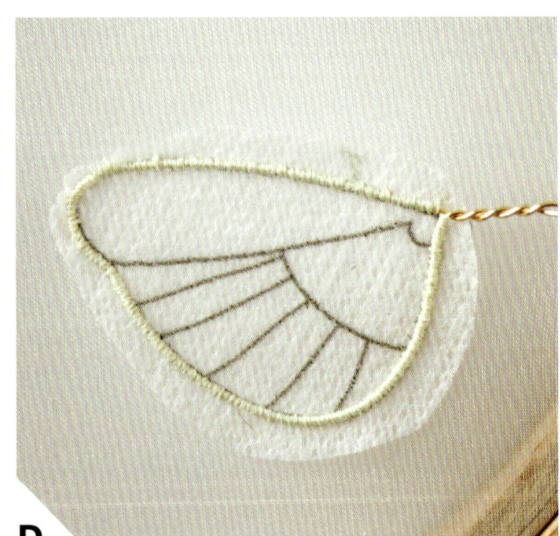

D

Embroider the Wings

Forewings

Stitch each forewing with 1 strand of DMC embroidery floss and a size 10 embroidery needle unless otherwise specified. The stitch direction starts at the inner corner and follows the curve of the wing.

1. Fill the top of the wing with long and short stitches of DMC 564 and 3815. Satin stitch the eye spot with DMC 369. **A**

A

· EMBROIDERING ON TRANSPARENT FABRIC ·

A portion of the wing will remain transparent, so take care to keep the backside of the embroidery tidy.

2. Split stitch the veins with DMC 10. Do not travel your thread across the back when moving from one wing vein to the next. Instead, tie off the end of the thread after completing each vein and begin a new thread at the start of the next vein. **B**

B

3. Repeat Steps 1–2 with other forewing.

Hindwings

Stitch each hindwing with 1 strand of DMC embroidery floss and a size 10 embroidery needle unless otherwise specified. The stitch direction starts at the inner corner and follows the curve of the wing.

1. Embroider the wing with long and short stitches of DMC 352, 353, and 369. **C**

C

2. Split stitch the veins with DMC 10. Do not travel your thread across the back when moving from one wing vein to the next. Instead, tie off the end of the thread after completing each vein and begin a new thread at the start of the next vein. **D**

D

3. Repeat Steps 1–2 with the other hindwing. **E**

4. Wash away the stitch stabilizer and lay the fabric flat to dry.

E

Embroider the Mantis

Use a size 10 embroidery needle and 1 strand of DMC stranded embroidery floss unless otherwise specified.

1. Secure both squares of KONA Everglade fabric in the 5¼˝ hoop with the body pattern on top.

Upper Legs

1. Fill in the legs with long and short stitches with DMC 10 and 472. Add straight stitches of DMC 841 at the joints of each leg segment. **A**

Lower Legs

1. Embroider straight stitches of DMC 10 and DMC 472 to fill in the lower legs. Add small straight stitches of DMC 841 at the joints of each leg segment. **B**

Body

See Needle-Felted Padding (page 34) for more information about felted padding.

1. Felt the body and head with the 38 gauge star-tipped felting needle and Corriedale wool roving. Use the Oats roving for the head and lower body. Use the Chartreuse roving for the center body section. Round the shapes to match the pattern. **C**

2. Retrieve the Praying Mantis pattern sticker set aside earlier. Remove the sticker's back and adhere the pattern to the fabric. Make sure that the pattern is aligned with the needle felted padding. **D**

3. Satin stitch the eyes with DMC 09 and the head with DMC 841. Backstitch the antennae with DMC 09. **E**

4. Embroider over the padded thorax with long and short stitches of DMC 3815 and stripes of 564. **F**

5. Embroider long and short stitches of DMC 353 over the padded abdomen. **G**

6. Back stitch the horizontal segments with DMC 352.

7. Wash away the stabilizer paper, and lay the fabric flat to dry. Secure the embroidery back into the embroidery hoop.

8. Embroider the cerci at the base of the abdomen with long and short stitches of DMC 3815, 564, and 10. **H**

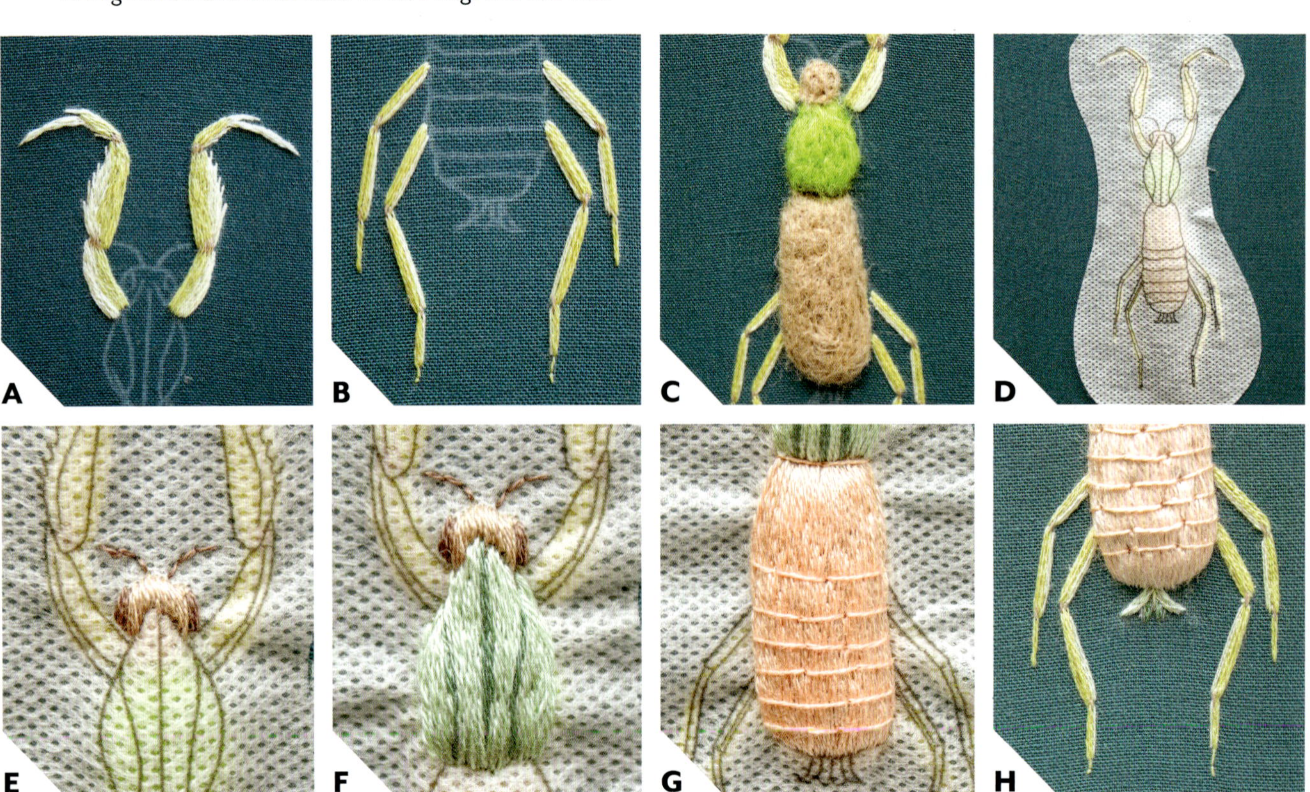

A B C D

E F G H

Assembly

See Wire Slips (page 38) for more information about cutting out, gluing, and attaching the wings to the body.

1. Cut away all excess fabric from the wings. Carefully apply fabric glue to the edges of the wings. Let the wings dry completely. **A**

2. Refer to the pattern and mark the 4 spots where the wings attach to the body with a pencil or air-soluble marker. Use the tapestry needle to make a hole in each spot. Attach the wings to the body by guiding the wire through the holes. Couch stitch the wings in place with DMC 564 at the inner corner of each wing. **B**

Finishing

See Displaying Embroidery (page 16) for instructions on how to secure your mantis in a hoop or in a frame. I transferred mine to an oval frame with a matching color palette.

A

B

Hedgehog in a Blueberry Wreath

FINISHED PROJECT SIZE: 5½˝ × 5½˝ (14 × 14cm)

This cheerful hedgehog is one of my favorite patterns in this book because it explores multiple stumpwork techniques and textures. The hedgehog's impressively realistic spines are created with a quick and simple method: padded applique with faux hedgehog fur. The appliqued fur blends seamlessly into the embroidered face and body for a natural look. Encircle the hedgehog with a wreath of entangled blueberry branches made from silk florals, thread-wrapped beads, and string padding for a charming finish.

Materials

- 6½˝ (16.5cm) embroidery hoop
- Size 8 and 10 embroidery needles
- Size 20 chenille needle
- Thread conditioner
- Jacquard Silk Colors Green Label: 735 Kelly Green, 736 Viridian Green, and 701 Citron
- Large round or mop watercolor brush
- Fabric stiffener
- Clover Needlecraft Mini Iron
- Benzie Design Corriedale wool roving: Swallow
- Benzie Design stuffing tool (optional)
- 12mm round wooden beads
- Chalk fabric pencil
- C&T Publishing Wash-Away Stitch Stabilizer paper
- Hedgehog pattern (page 151)
- Blueberry Leaves pattern (page 151)
- Frame or display hoop, optional

Fabric and Thread

- 2 squares 10˝ × 10˝ (25.4 × 25.4cm) of Sky Ombre by Jennifer Sampou for Robert Kaufman in Aloe
- 9˝ × 12˝ (22.9 × 30.5cm) sheet of Benzie Design wool felt in Toast
- 7˝ × 7˝ (17.8 × 17.8cm) square of silk habotai, white
- 6˝ × 6˝ (15.2 × 15.2cm) square of Steiff Schulte faux Hedgehog mohair fabric
- Bernat Cotton Solids Yarn in off-white
- The Thread Gatherer Silken Pearl size 5 #076 Chocolate Caramel
- Thread Gatherer Aurora #015 Olive Branch
- The Thread Gatherer's Sheep's Silk #019 in Toadie Green
- 1 skein each of the following DMC 6-stranded cotton embroidery floss colors

STITCHES USED IN THIS PROJECT

Couch Stitch, page 30

Satin Stitch, page 28

Straight Stitch, page 25

Long and Short Stitch, page 31

Back Stitch, page 26

Seed Stitch, page 25

Transfer the Pattern

See Transferring Patterns (page 23) for more information.

1. Print or trace the Hedgehog pattern onto Wash-Away Stitch Stabilizer. Follow the printing instructions on the package. Transfer the 3 body shape stickers to the Benzie wool felt. Set aside the other stickers. **A**

2. Cut out the felt shapes. **B**

3. Adhere the spines sticker to the back of the mohair fabric. **C**

4. Cut out the spines shape and remove the sticker. Set aside. **D**

Make the Padded Base

See Padding (page 33) for more information on felt padding.

1. Layer both squares of Aloe fabric into the 6½″ (16.5cm) hoop, and secure until drum-tight.

2. Couch stitch the smallest felt body shape (#1) to the center of the hooped fabric with a size 10 embroidery needle and 1 strand of DMC 841. Repeat with shapes #2 and #3, layering each piece over the previous one. **E**

3. Adhere the Hedgehog sticker to the fabric, aligning the body with the padded felt. **F**

Embroider the Hedgehog

Use a size 10 embroidery needle and 1 strand of DMC cotton embroidery thread unless otherwise specified.

Face

1. Satin stitch the eye with DMC 310. Add a seed stitch with DMC 3865 for a highlight. **A**

2. Satin stitch the nose with DMC 779. **B**

3. Beginning at the nose, fill in the snout with long and short stitches of DMC 841. Angle the stitches around the eye like a mask. Blend long and short stitches of DMC 3771 around the cheek area and 842 toward the spines. Stagger and overlap the stitches slightly to create a ruffled, fluffy fur look. Backstitch the mouth with DMC 779. **C**

Torso

1. Embroider the coat below the spine area with long and short stitches of DMC 3864 and 842. **D**

2. Embroider the belly with long and short stitches of DMC 841. **E**

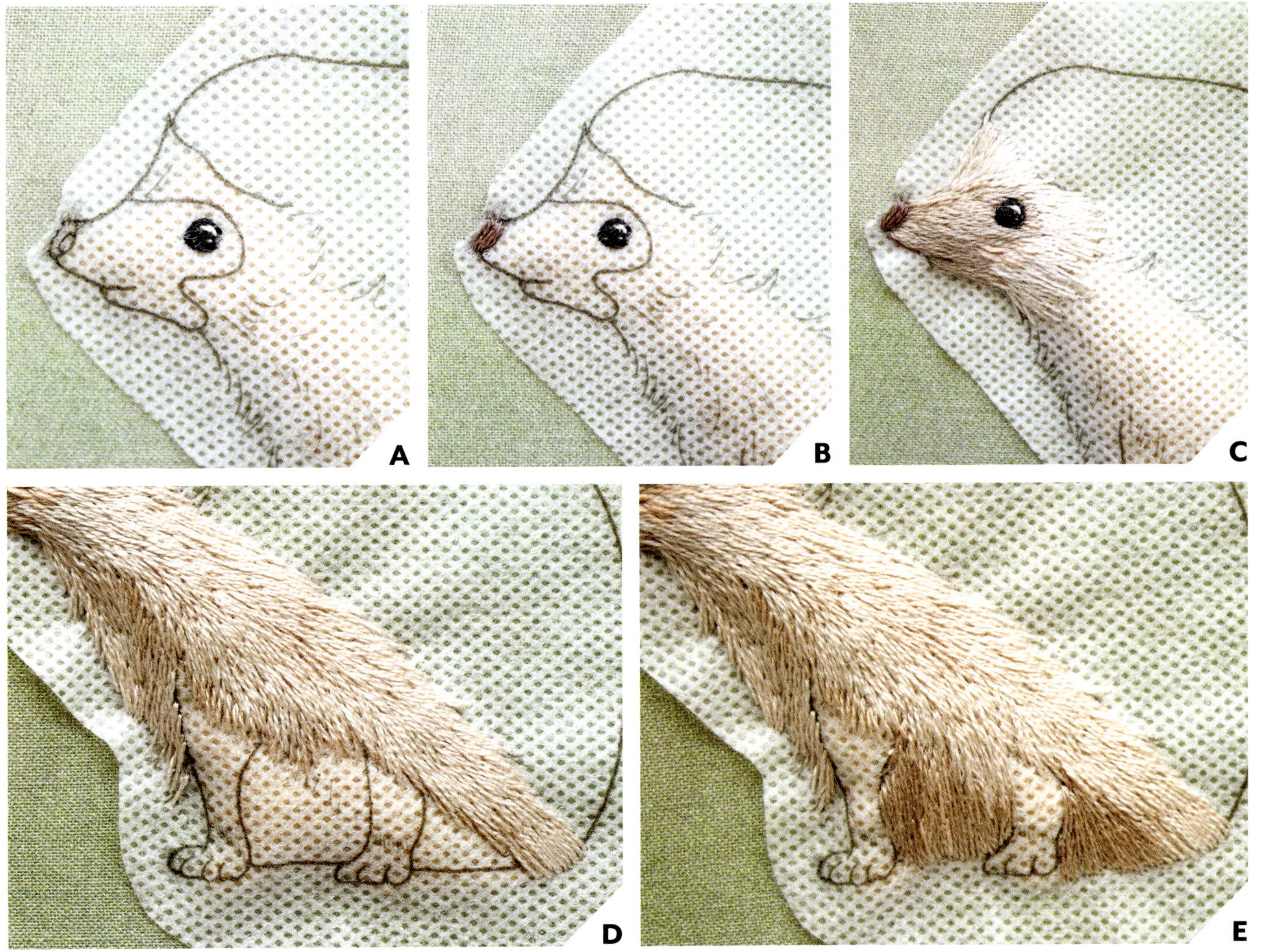

Legs

1. Fill the legs and paws with long and short stitches of DMC 948, 3771, and 841. Outline them with a backstitch of DMC 779. **A**

2. Add a single seed stitch of DMC 3865 to each toe to create claws. **B**

3. Wash away the stitch stabilizer, and lay the fabric flat to dry. Once dry, secure the fabric back in the hoop.

Attach the Spines

See Padded Applique (page 40) for more information. Use a size 10 needle and 1 strand of DMC 779 for this section.

1. Couch stitch the mohair fabric piece to the top of the hedgehog. Leave a 2˝ (5.1cm) opening. **C**

2. Stuff the applique with wool roving until firm. I used a stuffing tool so that the applique is filled evenly. **D**

3. Couch stitch the opening closed. **E**

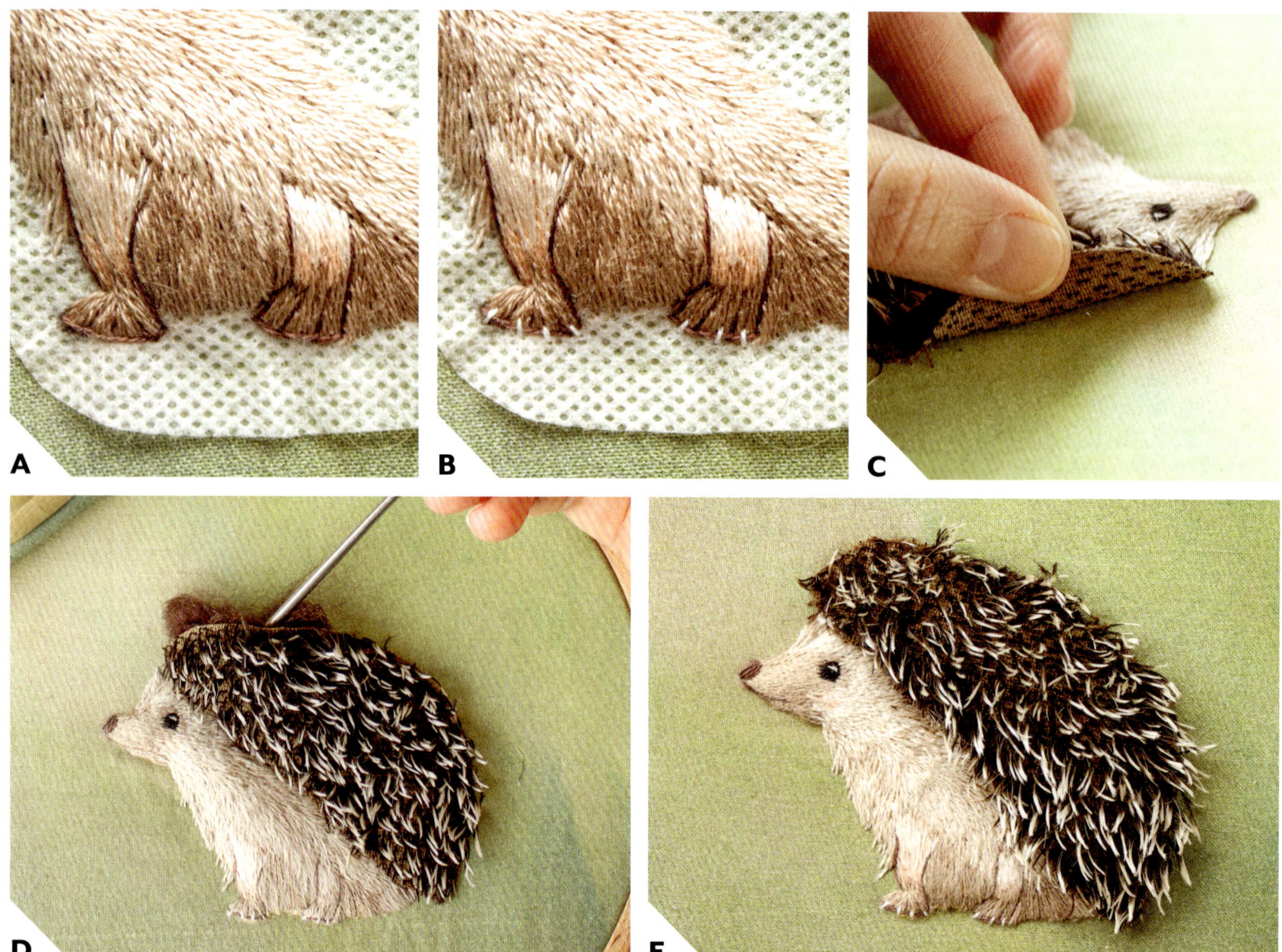

A B C D E

Make the Blueberry Wreath

See Stumpwork Techniques (page 32) for more information about thread-wrapped beads, string padding, and silk florals.

Branches

1. Couch stitch the Bernat cotton yarn in a wavy circle around the edge of the hoop, about 1¼″ (3.2cm) from the edge. Couch stitch over the yarn with The Thread Gatherer Silken Pearl Chocolate Caramel and the size 20 chenille needle (see String Padding, page 35). **A**

2. Lay and arrange the Thread Gatherer Aurora Olive Branch thread around the ring from Step 1. Couch stitch it down at random places along the string with 1 strand of DMC 731 and a size 10 embroidery needle. **B**

Leaves

1. Prepare the silk habotai with fabric stiffener and let dry (see Silk Botanicals, page 41). Paint the fabric with silk dyes, and let dry. Transfer each Blueberry Leaf pattern four times to the silk fabric using your preferred method. I used a white fabric chalk pencil. **C**

2. Cut out the leaves and press a vein down the center of each leaf with the Clover Mini Iron. **D**

3. Arrange the leaves around the string wreath. Straight stitch the base of each leaf with The Thread Gatherer's Sheep's Silk in Toadie Green and a chenille needle to attach the leaves around the wreath at random. **E**

Blueberries

1. Wrap 8 wooden beads with 3 strands of DMC 312 and a size 8 embroidery needle (see Wrapped Beads, page 42). Wrap 3 beads with 3 strands of DMC 3839.

2. Thread a size 8 needle with 3 strands of DMC 3750. Bring the needle under a few strands of thread at the end of one the darker blueberries. **A**

3. Move 1 mm over and bring the needle through again, catching a few threads. Pull the thread almost all the way through but stop when it creates a small loop. **B**

4. Continue making loops of thread that encircle the end of the blueberry. Overlap the loops slightly to create a ruffled texture.

5. Repeat Steps 1–4 with DMC 3838 to create loops of thread on the lighter unripened blueberries. **C**

6. Place the beads around the wreath. Attach each bead with a straight stitch at the base in a matching thread. Position some pairs of blueberries close together to form small clusters. **D**

Finishing

See Displaying Embroidery (page 16) for instructions on how to secure your hedgehog in a hoop or in a frame. I transferred mine to an ACMS needlework frame.

Goliath Flower Beetle

FINISHED PROJECT SIZE: 2″ × 2¼″ (5.1 × 5.7cm)

The dramatic colors and bold design of the Goliath Flower beetle make it a striking subject to embroider. This pattern combines needle felted padding, wire slips for the wings and wing covers, and thread painted details to recreate this unique beetle in lifelike detail. Pair the embroidered design with an ornate antique frame for a stunning finish.

Materials

- 4″ (10.2cm) embroidery hoop
- Size 8 and 10 embroidery needles
- Tapestry needle
- Thread conditioner
- 24 gauge jewelry wire
- Wire cutters
- Small, pointed scissors
- Fabric glue
- Craft-quality detail paint brush
- Benzie Design Corriedale wool roving: White
- 38 Gauge Cross Star felting needle
- Needle felting pad
- Water-away stitch stabilizer transfer paper
- Graphite transfer paper (black and white)
- Beetle Wings pattern (page 158)
- Beetle Wing Casings pattern (page 158)
- Beetle Body pattern (page 158)
- Beetle Thorax pattern (page 158)
- Frame or display hoop, optional

Fabric and Thread

- 2 squares 7″ × 7″ (17.8 × 17.8cm) of KONA cotton in Foxglove
- 6″ × 6″ (15.2 × 15.2cm) square KONA cotton in Black
- 6″ × 6″ (15.2 × 15.2cm) square of KONA cotton in Bordeaux
- Kreinik Very Fine Braid #4 005HL
- 1 skein each of the following DMC 6-stranded cotton embroidery floss colors

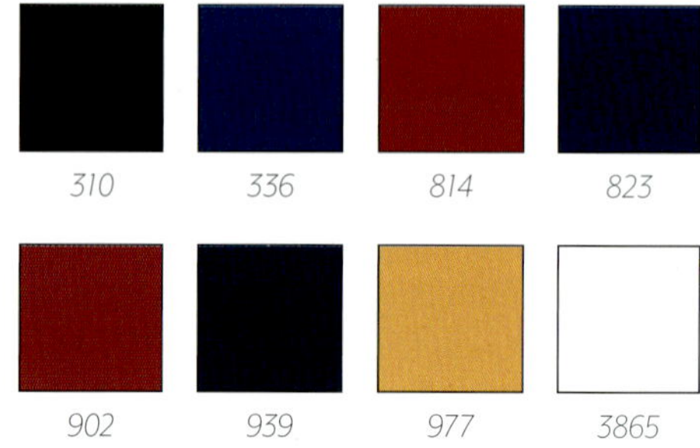

STITCHES USED IN THIS PROJECT

Couch Stitch, page 30
Long and Short Stitch, page 31
Back Stitch, page 26
Straight Stitch, page 25
Seed Stitch, page 25
Satin Stitch, page 28

Transfer the Pattern

See Transferring Patterns (page 23) for more information.

1. Transfer the Beetle Wings pattern onto the square of KONA Black using your preferred method. I used white graphite paper. Secure in the 4˝ (10.2cm) embroidery hoop. **A**

2. Transfer the Beetle Wing Casings pattern onto the square of KONA Bordeaux using your preferred method. I used white graphite paper. **B**

3. Transfer the Beetle Body pattern centered onto the square of KONA Foxglove using your preferred method. I used black graphite paper. **C**

4. Print or draw the Beetle Thorax pattern onto Wash-Away Stitch Stabilizer sticker paper. Follow the printing instructions on the package. Set aside the sticker for later.

Prepare the Wing Wire Slips

See Wire Slips (page 38) for more information.

1. Couch stitch the 24 gauge wire slips around the wings with DMC 310 and a size 10 needle until they are wrapped completely. Twist the wire ends together. **D**

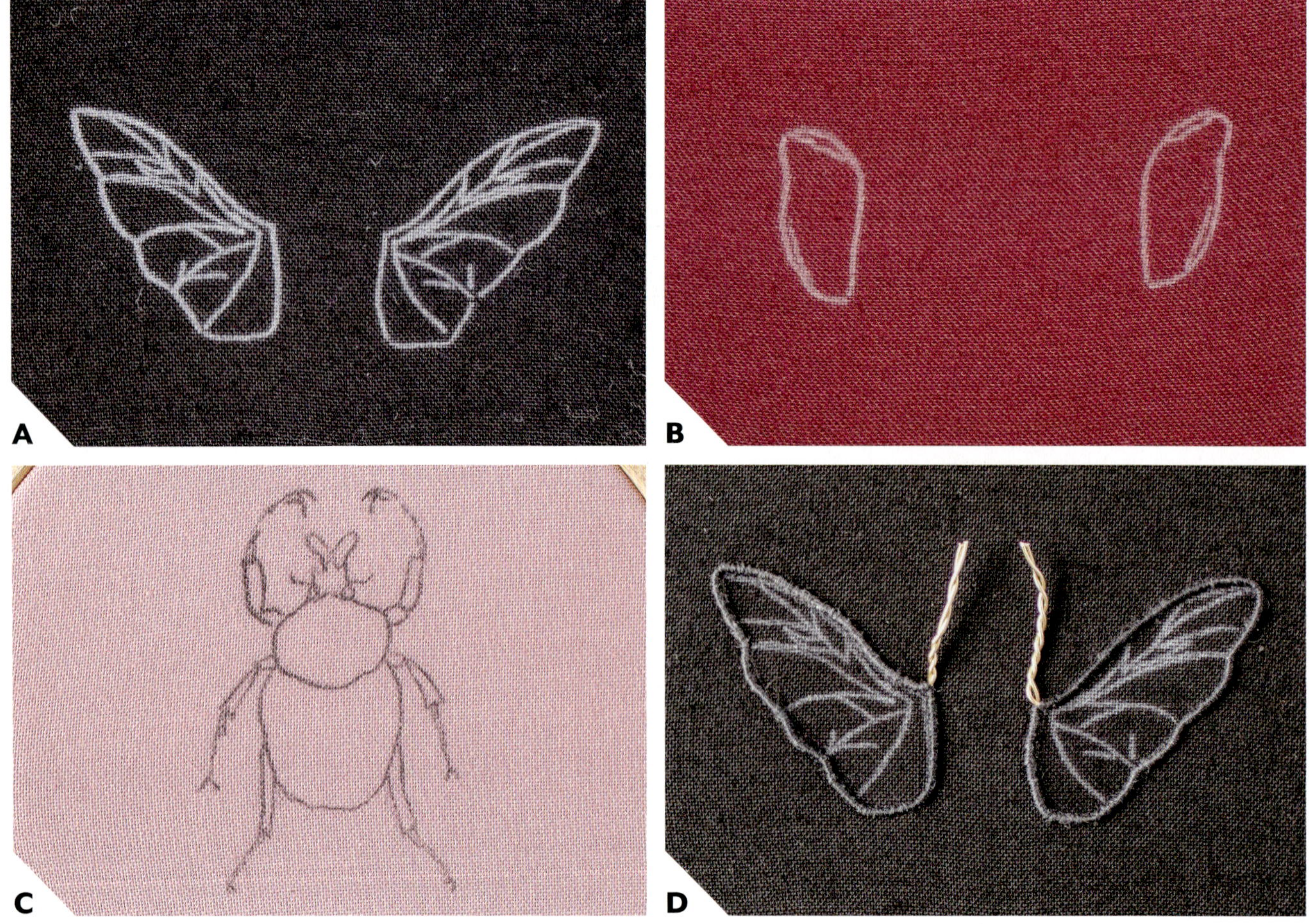

Embroider the Wings

Stitch the wings with 1 strand of DMC embroidery floss and a size 10 embroidery needle unless otherwise noted. The stitch direction starts at the inner corner and follows the curve of the wing.

1. Fill the inner corner of 1 wing with long and short stitches of DMC 310. **A**

2. Continue blending long and short stitches of DMC 939, 823, and 336 to fill the wing. Leave gaps for the wing veins. **B**

3. Backstitch the wing veins with Kreinik Very Fine Braid #4 005HL and a size 8 embroidery needle. **C**

4. Repeat Steps 1–3 to embroider the other wing.

Prepare the Wing Casing Wire Slips

See Wire Slips (page 38) for more information.

1. Switch the wing casings into the hoop. Cut 2 pieces of jewelry wire 2˝ (5.1cm) long. Couch stitch the wire pieces around the wing casings with DMC 902 until they are wrapped completely. The wire ends should meet with no excess wire. **D**

Embroider the Wing Casings

Stitch the wing casings with 1 strand of DMC embroidery floss and a size 10 embroidery needle. The stitch direction follows the curve of the wing casing.

1. Embroider long and short stitches of DMC 902 to fill the wing casings.

2. Add straight stitches and seed stitches of DMC 3865. **E-F**

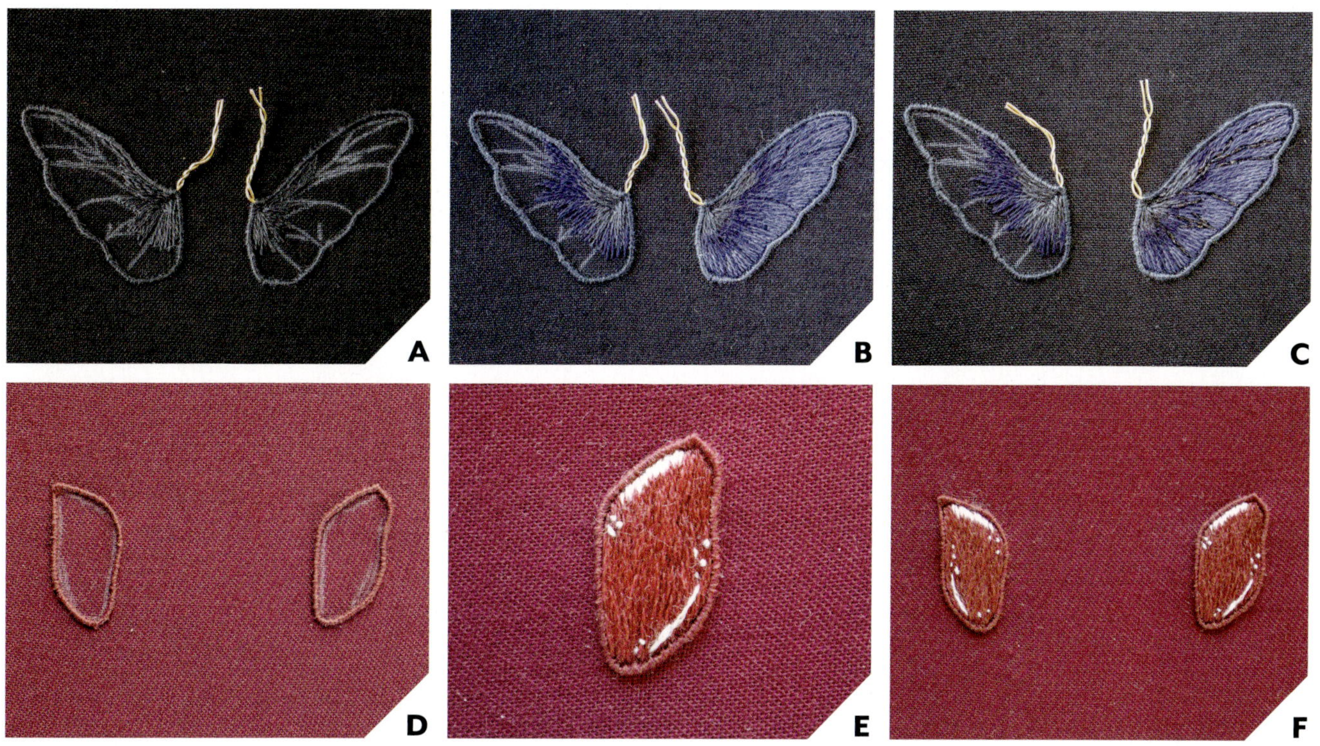

Prepare the Padded Base

See Needle-Felted Padding (page 34) for more information.

1. Layer the 2 pieces of KONA Foxglove with the body pattern on top into the hoop.

2. Felt the beetle's thorax and abdomen with the Corriedale wool roving and 38 star-tipped felting needle until each padded section is about ¼"-⅓" (7–8mm) tall and firm. The padding should be evenly rounded and smooth with a groove formed between the two body sections. Trim any flyaway fibers as needed. **A**

Embroider the Body

Stitch the body with 1 strand of DMC embroidery floss and a size 10 embroidery needle unless otherwise noted.

1. Embroider the eyes, head, and antenna with long and short stitches of DMC 310, 3865, and 336. **B**

2. Embroider the leg segments with satin and straight stitches of DMC 310. Add straight stitches of DMC 336 along the outer edge of each segment to create highlights. **C**

3. Create a fringe of straight stitches of DMC 977 on the inner side of the bottom legs. **D**

4. Retrieve the Beetle Thorax pattern sticker that was set aside earlier. Peel away the back of the sticker paper and adhere the pattern to the wool padding. **E**

5. Fill the stripes on the thorax with long and short stitches of DMC 310 and 3865. Embroider the abdomen with long and short stitches of DMC 814. Wash away the stitch stabilizer and let dry. **F**

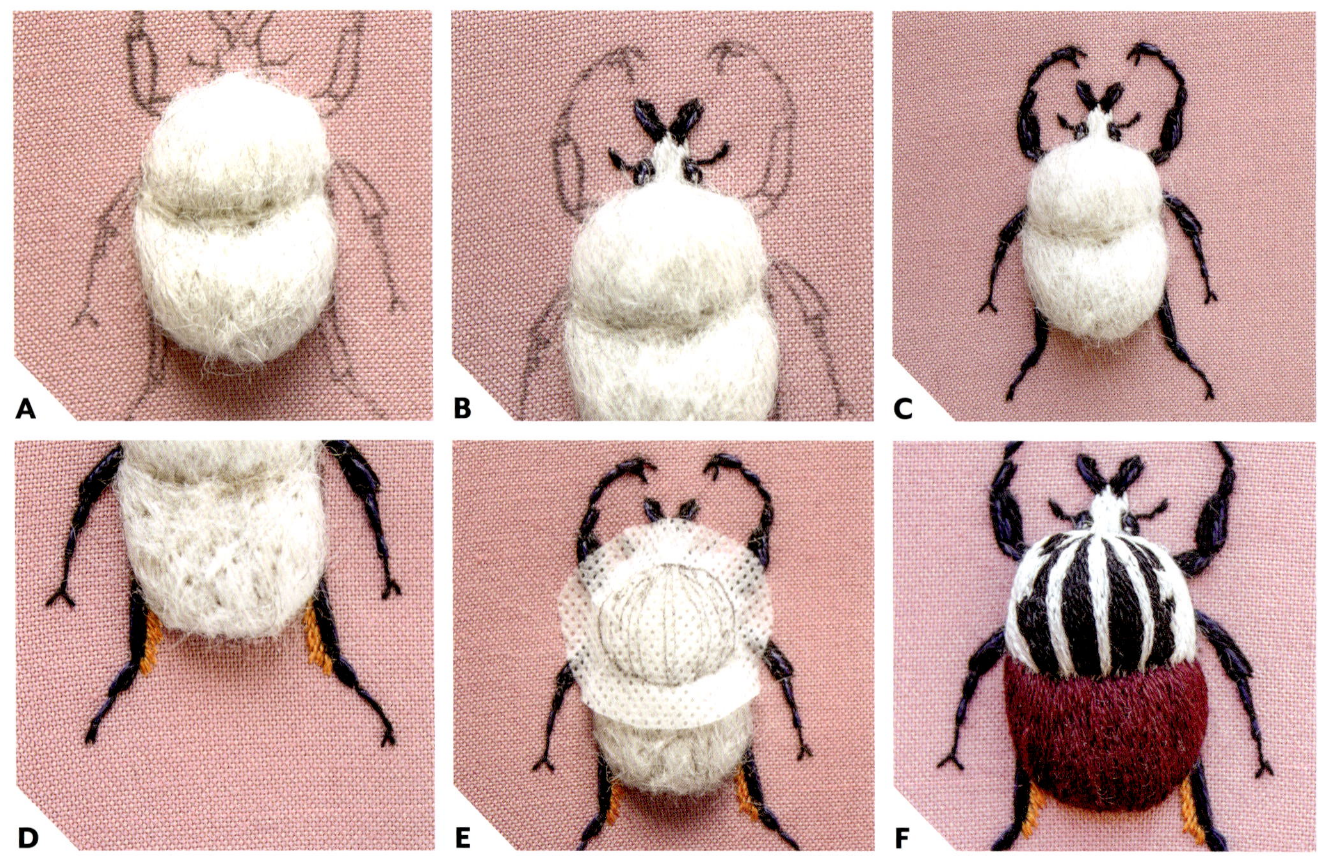

A

B

C

Assembly

See Wire Slips (page 38) for more information about cutting out, gluing, and attaching the wings to the body. Use a size 10 needle and 1 strand of DMC embroidery floss for this section.

1. Cut away all excess fabric from the wings. Paint glue onto the backs and edges of the wings. Let the wings dry completely. **A**

2. Repeat Step 1 with the wing casings. **B**

3. Refer to the pattern and mark the 4 spots where the wings and casings attach to the body with a pencil or air-soluble marker. Use the tapestry needle to make a hole in each spot. Attach the wings to the body by guiding the wire through the holes. Couch stitch through the inner corner of each wing to secure it in place with DMC 310.

4. Couch stitch the wing casings in place over the body with DMC 902. Stitch through the center of each casing and at random points around the edges. **C**

• ATTACHING WINGS •

When attaching layered wire slips, attach the lowest layer first. The lower wings of the beetle are partly covered up by the wing casings and should be attached first.

Finishing

See Displaying Embroidery (page 16) for instructions on how to secure your Goliath Flower Beetle in a hoop or in a frame. I transferred mine to a gilded vintage frame.

Tree Snail

FINISHED PROJECT SIZE: 1½˝ × 4¼˝ (3.8 × 10.8cm)

Snails are one of my favorite animals. These small and gentle creatures lead an unhurried life among the foliage. This pattern uses needle felted padding, wrapped wires, and beads to create the tree snail's life-like shell and eye stalks. Iridescent thread and glass beads add a shimmering, wet look to the snail's eye-catching trail. Finish this project as a jewelry box lid, or secure it in a hoop or frame for wall display.

Materials

7˝ (17.8cm) embroidery hoop

Size 10 and 7 embroidery needle

Size 10 beading needle

Tapestry needle

30 gauge paper-coated floral wire (white preferred)

Wirecutters

Scissors

Fabric glue

Benzie Design Corriedale wool roving: Latte, White

38 Gauge Cross Star felting needle

Needle felting pad

Miyuki Rocailles transparent crystal beads size #11

Czech glass seed beads, size #8 in crystal brown

Graphite transfer paper (black)

Tree Snail pattern (page 154)

Needlework jewelry box kit by SChandworks (optional)

Fabric and Thread

2 squares 10˝ × 10˝ (25.4 × 25.4cm) KONA cotton in Lilac

Kreinik Blending filament #1232HL

COSMO Nishikiito metallic thread #106

Gutterman sewing thread (white)

1 skein each of the following DMC 6-stranded cotton embroidery floss colors:

STITCHES USED IN THIS PROJECT

Satin Stitch, page 28

Long and Short Stitch, page 31

Back Stitch, page 26

Couch Stitch, page 30

Transfer the Pattern

See Transferring Patterns (page 23) for more information.

1. Transfer the snail pattern onto the square of KONA Lilac using your preferred method. I used black graphite paper. Secure both squares of KONA Lilac in the 7˝ (17.8cm) embroidery hoop. **A**

Prepare the Padded Base

See Needle-Felted Padding (page 34) for more information. Use the Corriedale wool roving in Latte and 38 star-tipped felting needle.

1. Felt the snail's tail until firm and evenly rounded. The felt padding should be 5mm tall and slope gently downward toward the slime trail.

2. Felt the snail's head until the padding is 5mm tall at the front and gradually reaches 1cm tall where the head meets the shell. The padding should be firm and evenly rounded. Leave the tentacles on the head unfelted. **B**

Embroider the Snail

Embroider the snail with a size 10 embroidery needle and 1 strand of DMC stranded embroidery floss unless otherwise specified.

Head

1. Embroider the tentacles and completely over the padded head with long and short stitches of DMC 05. **C**

2. Cut 2 pieces 2˝ (5.1cm) long of floral wire. Wrap ¾˝ (1.9cm) of both wires with 1 strand of DMC 05 (see Thread-Wrapped Wires, page 36).

3. Put a dot of fabric glue on the wrapped ends of each wire and adhere a size 8 crystal brown seed bead to the end. The bead should fit snugly over the wire. Let dry completely. **D**

4. Insert each eye stalk from Step 3 into the top of the snail's head. Use a tapestry needle to make a hole about ⅜˝ (1cm) above each tentacle. Thread the unwrapped ends of the wires through the holes until the exposed wire is covered. Couch stitch with DMC 05 at the base to secure the eye stalks in place. **E**

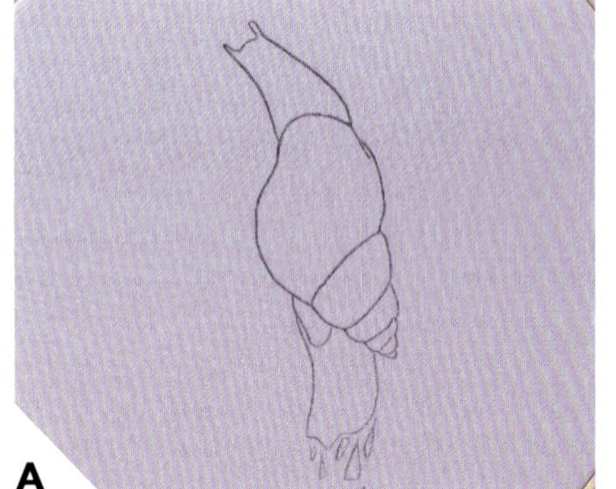

A

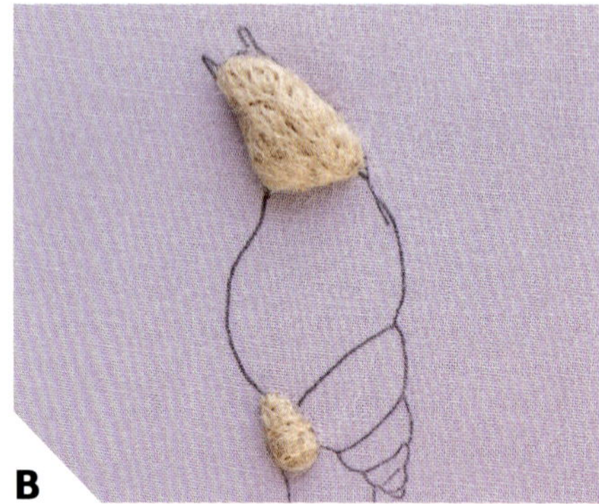

B

C

D

E

Tail

1. Embroider over the padded tail with long and short stitches of DMC 05. **A**

Embroider the Trail

1. Use long and short stitches of DMC 30 to fill the snail's trail. Thread the size 7 embroidery needle with Kreinik blending filament 1232HL, and add long and short stitches throughout the trail. **B**

2. Thread the beading needle with white Gutermann sewing thread. Attach the Miyuki Rocailles transparent crystal beads at random spots along the snail's trail to create bubbles. **C**

Embroider the Shell

1. Felt the shell with White Corriedale roving and the size 38 Star needle until firm and smoothly rounded. Begin with the largest shell section, and felt the wool until the shape is filled and the padding is ½" (1.2cm) tall. Felt the next shell section until the padding is ⅜" (1cm) tall. Each subsequent shell section should be felted just a couple millimeters shorter than the last, so that the shell's height slopes gently down toward the tail. **D**

· LAYERS OF DEPTH ·

Felt the padding at different heights within the same design to create more realistic layers of depth. In this pattern, the shell is felted at a greater height than the tail and head, and the tentacles and slime trail sit flush against the fabric to make the rest of the snail appear more three-dimensional.

A

B

C

D

2. Satin stitch the shell with the size 7 embroidery needle and 3 strands of the following DMC colors: 433, 780, 436, 3864, and 739. Use one color per shell section, going from dark to light. Backstitch between each shell section with COSMO Nishikiito #106 and the size 7 needle. **A-B**

Finishing

See Displaying Embroidery (page 16) for instructions on how to secure your snail in a hoop or in a frame. I transferred mine to a jewelry box lid using a mat board and the framing method.

The SCHandworks jewelry box is designed to display a custom embroidery piece. Lace the finished embroidery over the mat board. Secure the embroidery and mat board to the jewelry box lid with super glue. **C-D**

A

B

C

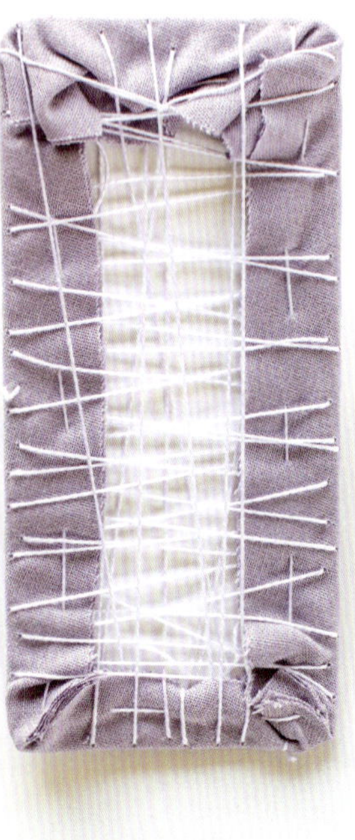
D

Tree Frog

FINISHED PROJECT SIZE: 2¼˝ × 3˝ (5.7 × 7.6cm)

When we lived along the Gulf coast, my family had a frequent visitor to our window each night: a small (and very loud) tree frog. This fascinating little creature brought us such immense joy with its vibrant coloring and exuberant croaking. I was inspired to stitch a two-sided replica where both sides of the design could be viewed. The two sides of this mirrored pattern are stitched separately and then attached together in a double-sided window frame for a unique finish. Display it on a tabletop or shelf where it can be appreciated from multiple angles.

Materials

- 5˝ (12.7cm) and 4˝ (10.2cm) embroidery hoops
- Size 10 embroidery needle
- Fabric glue
- Craft-quality detail paint brush
- Benzie Design Corriedale wool roving: Chartreuse
- 38 Gauge Cross Star felting needle
- Needle felting pad
- C&T Publishing Wash-Away Stitch Stabilizer paper
- Graphite transfer paper (black)
- Frog Topside pattern (page 150)
- Frog Underside pattern (page 150)

Fabric and Thread

- 7˝ × 7˝ (17.8 × 17.8cm) square of silk organza in white
- 2 squares 6˝ × 6˝ (15.2 × 15.2cm) of KONA cotton in Green Tea
- 1 skein each of the following DMC 6-stranded cotton embroidery floss colors:

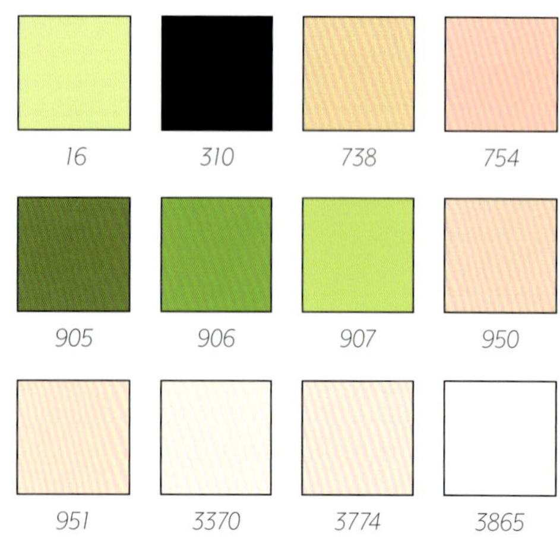

STITCHES USED IN THIS PROJECT

Satin Stitch, page 28
Long and Short Stitch, page 31
Seed Stitch, page 25
Straight Stitch, page 25

Transfer the Pattern

See Transferring Patterns (page 23) for more information. Please note that you will transfer the Frog Topside pattern twice for this project: once with the Wash-Away Stitch Stabilizer paper and once with graphite transfer paper.

1. Print or draw the Frog Topside and Frog Underside patterns onto the Wash-Away Stitch Stabilizer paper. Follow the printing instructions on the package. Set aside the Frog Topside sticker for later.

2. Remove the back of the Frog Underside pattern sticker and adhere it to the square of silk organza. Secure the fabric in the 5˝ (12.7cm) embroidery hoop. **A**

3. Transfer *another* copy of the Frog Topside pattern to the square of KONA cotton Green Tea using your preferred transfer method. I use graphite transfer paper. Secure both fabric squares in the 4˝ (10.2cm) embroidery hoop. **B**

Prepare the Padded Base

See Needle-Felted Padding (page 34) for more information.

1. Felt the Corriedale wool roving with the 38 star-tipped felting needle to fill the shape of the frog until the padding is very firm and smooth. Build up the felted area where the frog's natural anatomy would be higher, such as the head and back.

The padded back should be about ⅝˝ (1.6cm) tall and gently rounded to emphasize the frog's curved belly. The felted arms and legs should slope downward from the back, reaching about 5mm in height. Use only a small pinch of wool to felt each narrow toe. The padded head and bottom should both sit about ⅜˝ (1cm) tall, just slightly shorter than the frog's back. Trim any stray fibers for an even finish. **C**

• FELTING WITHIN THE LINES •

It is important to felt within the lines of this pattern, especially within the legs and toes. If the padding strays over the lines, the two sides of the frog will not align properly at the assembly stage.

A

B

C

Embroider the Underside

Embroider this pattern with a size 10 embroidery needle and 1 strand of DMC cotton embroidery floss unless otherwise specified.

Head

1. Fill the eye with long and short stitches of DMC 310 and 738. Add a couple of seed stitches of DMC 3865 to the right side of the eye to create a highlight. A

2. Blend long and short stitches of DMC 905, 906, 907, and 16 to fill the side of the frog's face. The colors should create an ombre effect with the lightest color, 16, closest to the chin. Outline the shape of the chin with long and short stitches of DMC 950 and blend long and short stitches of DMC 3770 to fill the rest of the chin. B

Body

1. Continue stitching down the body from the chin. Blend long and short stitches of DMC 950 and 3770 to fill the frog's belly. Embroider the side of the belly with long and short stitches of 905, 906, 907, and 16. C

2. Embroider the arms and fingers with long and short stitches of DMC 3770, 951, 3774, and 754. D

3. Embroider the legs and feet with long and short stitches of DMC 3770, 950, 3774, and 754. E

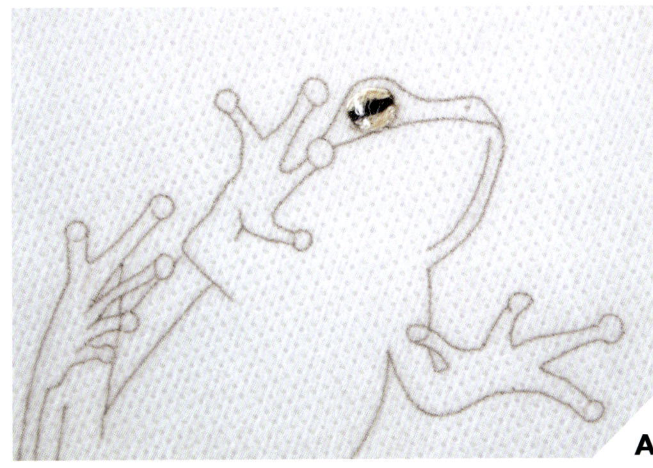
A

B

C

D

E

Embroider the Topside

Embroider this pattern with a size 10 embroidery needle and 1 strand of DMC cotton embroidery floss unless otherwise specified.

1. Retrieve the Frog Topside pattern sticker. Remove the sticker back from the pattern and adhere it to the needle felted body. Make sure that the pattern aligns with the padded shape underneath. **A**

Head

1. Fill the eye with long and short stitches of DMC 310 and 738. Add a couple of small seed stitches of DMC 3865 to the right side of the eye to create a highlight. **B**

2. Beginning at the nose, blend long and short stitches of DMC 905, 906, and 16 to fill the head. Continue downward to fill the back with long and short stitches of DMC 906, 907, 16, and 950 with the colors gradually becoming lighter as they reach the belly. **C**

3. Embroider the tympanum with satin stitches of DMC 738. **D**

Arms and Legs

1. Begin at the frog's shoulders and blend long and short stitches of DMC 906 into the top of each arm. Create an ombre effect by blending long and short stitches of DMC 907 and 16 to fill the rest of the arm and tops of the toes. End each toe with long and short stitches of DMC 738 and 951. **E**

2. Repeat Step 1 and embroider the back legs and toes with long and short stitches of DMC 906, 907, 16, 738, and 951. **F**

Assembly

1. Cut out the topside of the frog. Take care to cut up to but not into the stitching.

• EASING COMMON CONCERNS ABOUT CUTTING •

Cutting so close to a finished embroidery is sure to draw apprehension! Be assured that the embroidery will not fall apart. The needle felted padding provides a structural barrier to prevent the fabric from fraying and the embroidery thread from unraveling at the edges of the design. Wire slips and layered felt padding act in the same way. The cut-out design will hold up under handling, so do not fret about this step of the process.

2. Apply a thin layer of fabric glue to the edges of the frog with a fine paintbrush. Smooth down the edges. Trim away any remaining fabric fibers after the glue has dried. **A**

3. Apply a thin layer of fabric glue to the backside of the cut-out frog, and carefully align it opposite the underside view (still in the hoop). Let dry completely, adhering the frog top and underside.

4. Secure the frog by blending a couple of small straight stitches of DMC 754 through each of the toes on each side. Bring the needle through both layers of the frog to anchor the feet in place. **B**

Finishing

See Displaying Embroidery (page 16) for more information about finishing your embroidery. I finished my frog in a window frame that can be viewed from both sides. The finished embroidery is gently stretched (careful not to tear the organza) and secured with super glue between the two fitted pieces of the frame. I trimmed away any excess fabric from the edges of the frame once the glue had dried.

FLORA

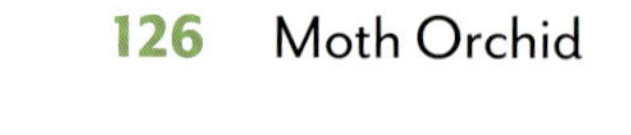

Oak Branch

FINISHED PROJECT SIZE: 3½″ × 5″ (8.9 × 12.7cm)

I grew up in a neighborhood named for its numerous oaks, and so these beautiful trees hold a special place in my heart. Now that I move around the country a lot, I am always amazed at the wide variety and differences in oak trees from one area to the next. Still, the familiar form of an acorn remains the same across the world. This pattern combines silk florals, thread-wrapped wires and beads, and three-dimensional stitches to create a simple yet elegant oak branch that honors the timeless beauty and resilience of this ancient species.

Materials

- 5¼″ (13.3cm) embroidery hoop
- Size 18 chenille needle
- 2 gauge paper-coated floral wire (brown)
- 24 gauge paper-coated floral wire (green)
- Wire cutters
- Beacon Fabri-Tac fabric glue
- Jacquard Silk Green Label Dyes: 701 Citron, 735 Kelly Green, and 736 Viridian Green
- Colored pencils (Castle Arts Soft-Touch)
- Large round mop or watercolor brush
- Fabric stiffener
- Fixative spray, such as Krylon Workable Fixatif
- Clover Needlecraft Mini Iron
- Bohin fabric chalk pencil (white)
- 15mm oval egg-shaped wood beads
- Oak Leaves pattern (page 155)
- Frame or display hoop, optional

Fabric and Thread

- 8″ × 8″ (20.3 × 20.3cm) Mary Jo Hiney Silk Velvet in Forget-Me-Knot blue
- 7″ × 7″ (17.8 × 17.8cm) silk habotai, white
- 1 skein each of the following The Thread Gatherer Silk Pearl size 5 colors: 243 Woods of Gold and 076 Chocolate Caramel
- 1 skein of The Thread Gatherer Silken Chenille in 426 Quartersawn Oak
- 1 skein of DMC 6-stranded cotton embroidery floss in the following color

472

· CHANGING SEASONS ·

You can change out the green silk dye colors with #706 Apricot, #710 Poppy Red, #745 Brown Sienna, #750 Chocolate Brown to recreate the colors of oak leaves in autumn. Couch stitch the wire with a brown thread and swap out the blue velvet background for a forest or moss green fabric to complement the orange and brown tones of the leaves.

STITCHES USED IN THIS PROJECT

Couch Stitch, page 30

John James
Pebble

Prepare the Fabric

See Silk Botanicals (page 41) for more information on preparing silk fabric.

1. Treat the silk habotai with the fabric stiffener and let dry. Paint the fabric with the silk fabric dyes using a watercolor brush. **A**

Transfer the Pattern

See Transferring Patterns (page 23) for more information.

1. Transfer the Oak Leaves pattern onto the square of dyed silk habotai using your preferred method. I used a chalk pencil. Secure in the 5¼˝ (13.3cm) embroidery hoop. **B**

Make the Leaves

1. Thread the size 10 needle with 1 strand of DMC 472. Couch stitch the 24 gauge floral wire to the center vein of the leaves, extending it past the wire to create the stem. **C**

2. Cut out the leaves. Add details, such as veins and discoloration, with colored pencils in shades of green, yellow, and brown. Spray with the fixative spray, and let dry. **D**

· DRAWING ON FABRIC ·

Fabric treated with a fabric stiffener will behave like a canvas or paper. Oil and chalk pastels, paint, crayons, and colored pencils are all suitable mediums for marking on treated fabric. Be sure to spray the drawn-on fabric with a fixative to preserve the artwork and prevent smudging.

3. Use the Clover mini iron with the spade-shaped tip to add creases to the fabric along the vein lines. **E**

Make the Acorns

Acorns

See Beads (page 42) for more information about bead wrapping.

1. Thread the chenille needle with the The Thread Gatherer Silken Chenille in Quartersawn Oak.

2. Wrap the oval beads with the silken chenille thread. **A**

Caps

1. Cut a length of The Thread Gatherer Silk Pearl Chocolate Caramel approximately 50˝ (1.27m) long. Thread both ends through the size 18 chenille needle. **B**

• THREAD LENGTH •

Working with a long thread length is usually not advisable. In this case, the long thread length is necessary to complete the cap without having to change out the thread and disrupt the stitch pattern.

2. Place the acorn against the looped end of the thread. Bring the needle through the loop. **C**

3. Pull the thread taut to create a knot around the center of the acorn. **D**

4. Wrap the thread clockwise around the backside of the acorn until it meets at the knot again. **E**

5. Bring the needle down between the acorn and the thread wraps. **F**

6. Bring the needle up through the loop that forms. **G**

7. Gently pull the thread taut to create the stitch. **H**

Silk chenille has a velvety sheen that nicely mimics the look of a glossy acorn.

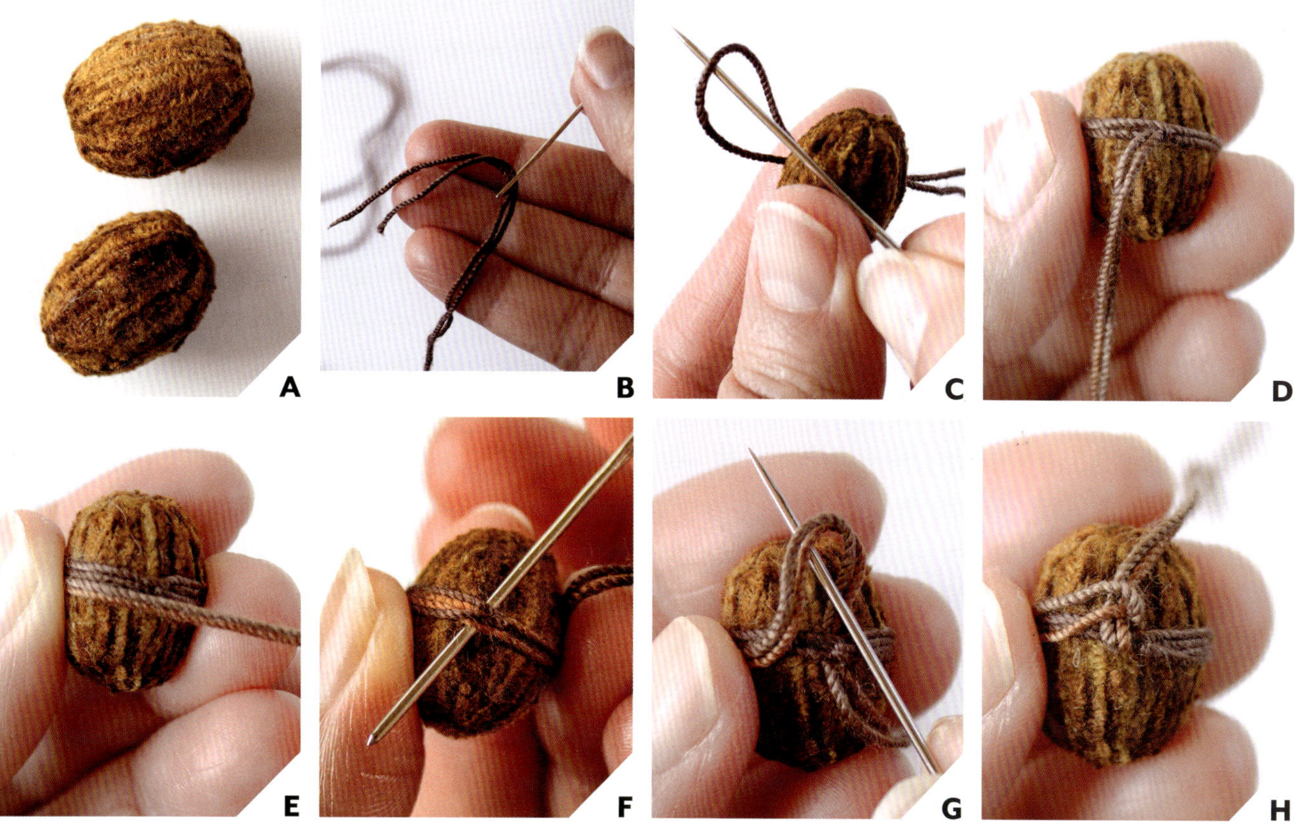

8. Move to the right of the stitch from Step 7, and repeat Steps 5–7 to create a second stitch. Continue until the row of stitches reaches around the acorn and back to the first stitch. I

9. Continue the stitch pattern and make another row of stitches above the first. To make the first downward stroke, bring the needle through the top of the loop of the first row. J

10. Continue creating the new row of stitches until you reach the top. Each row will have fewer stitches. K

11. Tie off the thread at the top of the acorn with a simple knot to secure the thread. L

12. Repeat Steps 1–11 for the other 2 acorns. M

Assembly

See Wires (page 36) for more information on thread wrapped wires.

1. Cut a 3¼˝ (8.3cm) piece of 2 gauge floral wire. Wrap the wire with The Thread Gatherer Silk Pearl Woods of Gold thread. Attach the leaves at various points along the wire. Cover the whole wire. N

2. Secure the velvet fabric in the 5¼˝ (13.3cm) embroidery hoop. O

3. Thread the chenille needle with the Woods of Gold silk pearl thread. Attach the branch to the velvet fabric with couching stitches along the branch. P

Q

R

4. Thread the chenille needle with the Chocolate Caramel silk pearl thread. Attach the acorns to the branch with couching stitches at the base of each cap. **Q-R**

Finishing

See Displaying Embroidery (page 16) for instructions on how to secure your oak branch in a hoop or in a frame. I transferred my branch to a vintage oval-shaped frame.

Blackberry Bramble

FINISHED PROJECT SIZE: 8″ × 8½″ (20.3 × 21.6cm)

Beads are a fun and easy way to incorporate color and texture into embroidery. This pattern uses beaded slips to create rounded, lifelike blackberries and simple stitched beading to add sparkling dew to the leaves and spider web. Display this piece near a light source to fully appreciate its sparkle.

Materials

3 embroidery hoops, sizes 4″ (10.2cm), 5¼″ (13.3cm), and 9″(22.9cm)

Size 9 embroidery needle

Size 18 chenille needle

Size 10 beading needle

Thread conditioner

2 gauge paper-coated floral wire (green)

26 gauge paper-coated floral wire (green)

Wire cutters

Scissors

Benzie Design Corriedale wool roving: Black, Chartreuse

Merino wool for filling

Clover mini iron

Jacquard Silk Green Label Dyes: 701 Citron, 735 Kelly Green, 736 Viridian Green

Large round or mop watercolor brush

Fabric stiffener

Bohin chalk pencil (white)

Miyuki Rocailles clear glass beads size #11

Miyuki glass clear transparent fringe beads size #8

Czech glass seed beads size #8 in the following colors: opaque mint green, opaque wasabi green, clear brown-lined, transparent ruby, transparent tortoise brown, opaque black, opaque terra dyed rose

Graphite tracing paper (white)

Large Blackberry pattern (page 152)

Small Blackberry pattern (page 152)

Blackberry Leaves pattern (page 152)

Spiderweb pattern (page 152)

Frame or display hoop, optional

Thread and Fabric

2 squares 12″ × 12″ (30.5 × 30.5cm) of KONA cotton in Bordeaux

7″ × 7″ (17.8 × 17.8cm) square of KONA cotton in Black

6″ × 6″ (15.2 × 15.2cm) square of KONA cotton in Summer Pear

9″ × 7″ (22.9 × 17.8cm) rectangle of silk habotai

The Thread Gatherer Silken Pearl Size 5 Lizard Back

Gutermann polyester sewing thread in Black

Gutterman polyester sewing thread in White

Gutterman polyester sewing thread in #305 petal pink

Kreinik Blending filament #093

1 skein of the following DMC 6-strand embroidery floss in the following color

472

STITCHES USED IN THIS PROJECT

Couch Stitch, page 30

Back Stitch, page 26

Straight Stitch, page 25

Transfer the Pattern

See Transferring Patterns (page 23) for more information.

1. Transfer the Spiderweb pattern to a square of the KONA Bordeaux fabric using your preferred method. I used white graphite tracing paper. Layer a second piece of KONA Bordeaux fabric underneath and secure both layers together in the 9″(22.9cm) hoop. **A**

2. Transfer 5 copies of the Large Blackberry pattern onto the KONA Black with white graphite paper. Secure in the 5¼″ (13.3cm) embroidery hoop. **B**

3. Transfer 3 copies of the Small Blackberry pattern onto the KONA Summer Pear fabric and secure in the 4″ (10.2cm) embroidery hoop. **C**

Embroider the Spiderweb

Embroider the web with a size 9 embroidery needle and the Kreinik blending filament #093.

1. Embroider the framework and radial threads of the spider web with backstitch. **D**

2. Embroider the hub (center) and spiral threads of the spider web with backstitch. **E**

3. Remove the embroidery from the hoop and gently hand wash it to remove any part of the transferred design that is not completely covered by the thin thread. Lay flat to dry. Secure the spider web back in the embroidery hoop.

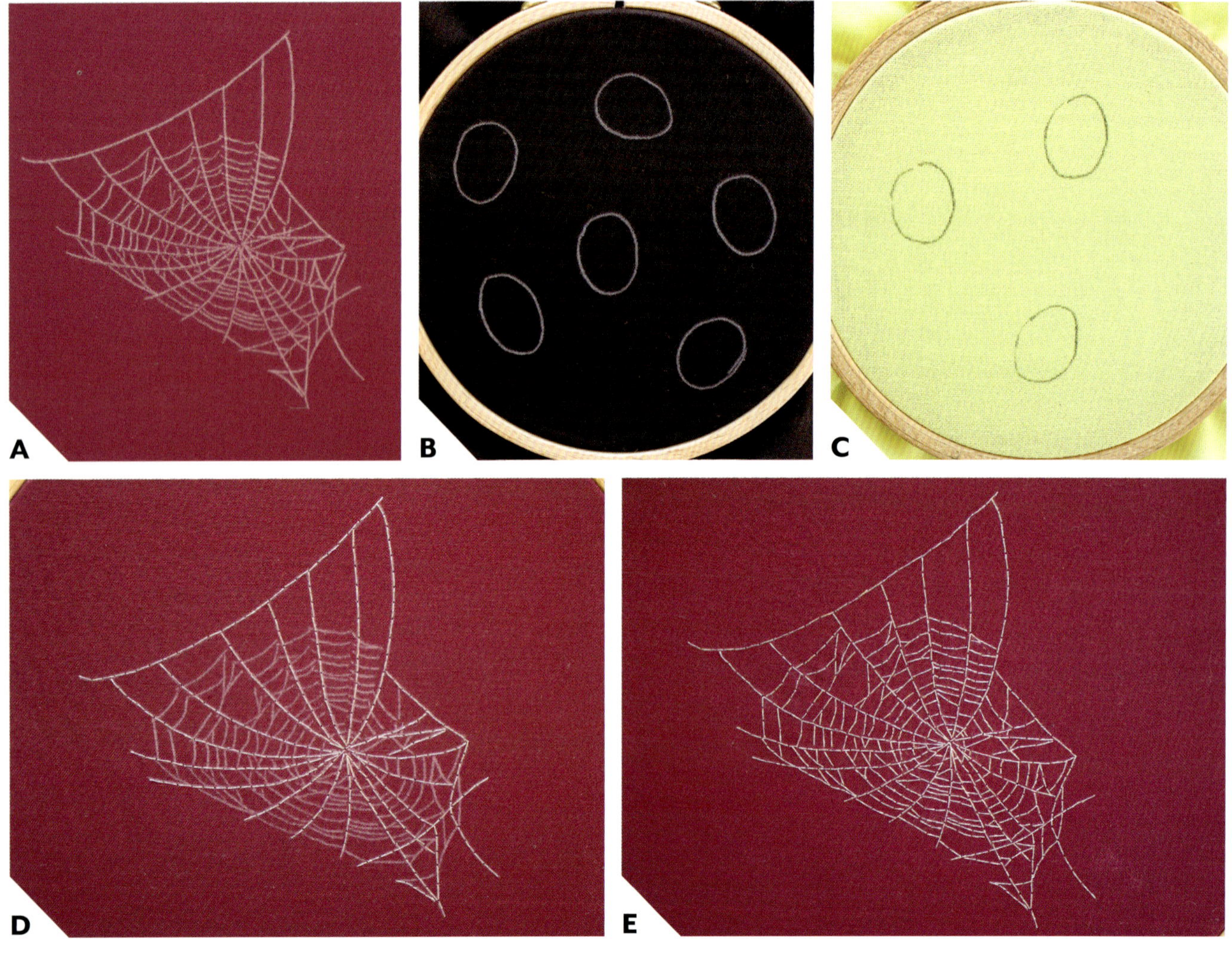

Embroider the Water Drops

1. Thread the size 10 beading needle with white sewing thread. Attach the size #11 clear Rocailles beads to the spider web to mimic water drops. Attach the beads at junctures throughout the spirals and along the radial threads of the web. **A**

· BEAD PLACEMENT ·

Beads that are spaced too evenly apart will appear less realistic. Position the beads at random, with some close together or nearly touching, for a more natural look.

A

B

Embroider the Blackberry Bramble

Branch

See Thread-Wrapped Wires (page 36) for more information.

1. Cut 3 stems from the 2 gauge floral wire: 7˝ (17.8cm), 4½˝ (11.4cm), and 4¼˝ (10.8cm). Cut 2 of each of the following sizes from the 26 gauge floral wire: 1½˝ (3.8cm), 2˝ (5.1cm), and 3˝ (7.6cm).

2. Wrap the 6 smaller stems with 2 strands of DMC 472. Leave only ⅜˝ (1cm) of each wire uncovered.

3. Wrap the 3 larger stems with The Thread Gatherer Silken Pearl Size 5 Lizard Back. As you cover them completely, attach the smaller stems on both sides, as shown. **B**

4. Thread the size 18 chenille needle with the Silken Pearl Lizard Back. Attach each branch to the web with couching stitches along the length of the main wrapped wire. Manipulate/bend the wire so that it meets the outer anchoring threads of the web. **C**

· EXTENDING THE WEB ·

If needed, extend the anchoring threads of the web to meet the branches by adding more backstitches of the Kreinik blending filament.

C

Leaves

See Silk Botanicals (page 41) for more information about silk florals.

1. Prepare the silk habotai with fabric stiffener, and let dry. Use a large round or mop watercolor brush and the Viridian Green fabric dye to paint loosely defined areas of color onto the fabric. Paint the Kelly Green and Citron dyes in the remaining spaces, allowing them to blend at the edges and create a subtle ombre. Let the fabric dry.

2. Transfer the Blackberry Leaves pattern 5 times onto the fabric with a chalk pencil or carbon paper. **A**

3. Cut out the leaves, and press a vein down the center of each leaf with the Clover Mini Iron. **B**

4. Thread a size 9 embroidery needle with 1 strand of DMC 472. Arrange the leaves on the ends of the branches. Backstitch 2 to 3 stitches at the base of each leaf to attach them to the branches. Place the leaves at random. **C**

A

B

C

Berries

See Beaded Slips (page 43) for detailed instructions on creating beaded slips. Embroider the beaded slips with a beading needle and Gutermann sewing thread. Strengthen the thread with thread conditioner.

1. Fill the large oval patterns on the black fabric with beads and the black sewing thread. Use primarily opaque black beads to fill the shape, but randomly place tortoise shell brown, translucent purple, and translucent red beads throughout each oval. **A**

• SEWING THREAD ALTERNATIVES •

You can substitute other thread you have on hand, such as DMC 6-stranded cotton embroidery thread, when making the beaded slips. Remember to match the thread to the bead color so it is less visible.

2. Fill the small oval patterns on the green fabric with beads and the pink sewing thread. Use opaque mint green and opaque wasabi green beads to fill most of the oval. Add some clear brown-lined and opaque terra dyed rose beads at random to mimic the ripening sections of the berry. **B**

3. Cut out the beaded slips. Leave a margin of fabric around each shape. With the corresponding sewing thread color and size 9 needle, gather each beaded slip with a running stitch. Use a small pinch of Corriedale roving to stuff each slip. **C**

4. Use a size 9 embroidery needle and corresponding sewing thread to attach each blackberry to the branch and leaves. Bring the needle up through the center of each berry and make a small straight stitch through the berry to couch it to the fabric. Repeat with several stitches for each berry until they are secure. **D**

A

B

C

D

Finishing Details

3-D Spider Web

1. Thread a size 9 embroidery needle with the Kreinik blending filament. Bring the thread up from behind a leaf, berry, or branch. **A**

2. Wrap the thread around a nearby branch once, and gently pull the thread taut. **B**

• SLIDING DEW DROPS •

Thread beads onto the needle between Steps 1 and 2 to add dew drops to the strands of web. These beads will slide freely along the strand for a fun interactive detail.

3. Stretch the thread 1–3˝ (2.5-7.6cm) to another three-dimensional anchoring point, and bring the needle down through the fabric to secure in place. **C**

4. Repeat Steps 1–3 to add three-dimensional strands of spiderweb to the berries and branches. **D**

Leaf Water Droplets

See Beads (page 42) for more information.

1. Thread a beading needle with white sewing thread. Add clear Miyuki glass fringe beads to the ends of the downturned leaves to mimic water drops rolling off the leaves. **E**

A B C D E

Finishing

See Displaying Embroidery (page 16) for instructions on how to secure your blackberry bramble in a hoop or in a frame. I transferred my embroidery to a Nurge display hoop.

Moth Orchid

FINISHED PROJECT SIZE: 3½˝ × 5˝ (8.9 × 12.7cm)

Orchids are one of my favorite flowers. Their vibrant colors, unique flower shape, and twisting aerial roots make them an interesting subject to embroider. This pattern provides an opportunity to explore several stumpwork techniques to create a standalone object, including: wire slips, thread-wrapped beads, and thread-wrapped wires.

Materials

- 4˝ (10.2cm) and 6¼˝ (15.9cm) embroidery hoops
- Sizes 8, 9, and 10 embroidery needles
- Size 18 chenille needle
- Thread conditioner
- 24 gauge jewelry wire
- 30 gauge jewelry wire
- 24 gauge paper-coated floral wire (green)
- 2 gauge paper-coated floral wire (green)
- Wire cutters
- Small, pointed scissors
- Fabric glue
- Super glue (optional)
- Craft-quality detail paint brush
- Benzie Design Corriedale wool roving: Fern
- Round wooden beads in sizes 12mm, 10mm, and 8mm (1 each)
- C&T Publishing Wash-Away Stitch Stabilizer paper
- Moth Orchid pattern (page 154)
- Mat board
- 2˝ (5.1cm) flower pot or similar vessel

Fabric and Thread

- 8˝ × 8˝ (20.3 × 20.3cm) square of silk organza in white
- 2 squares 6˝ × 6˝ (15.2 × 15.2cm) of KONA cotton in Doeskin
- 1 skein of The Thread Gatherer Aurora #016 Desert Moss
- 1 skein each of the following DMC 6-stranded cotton embroidery floss colors

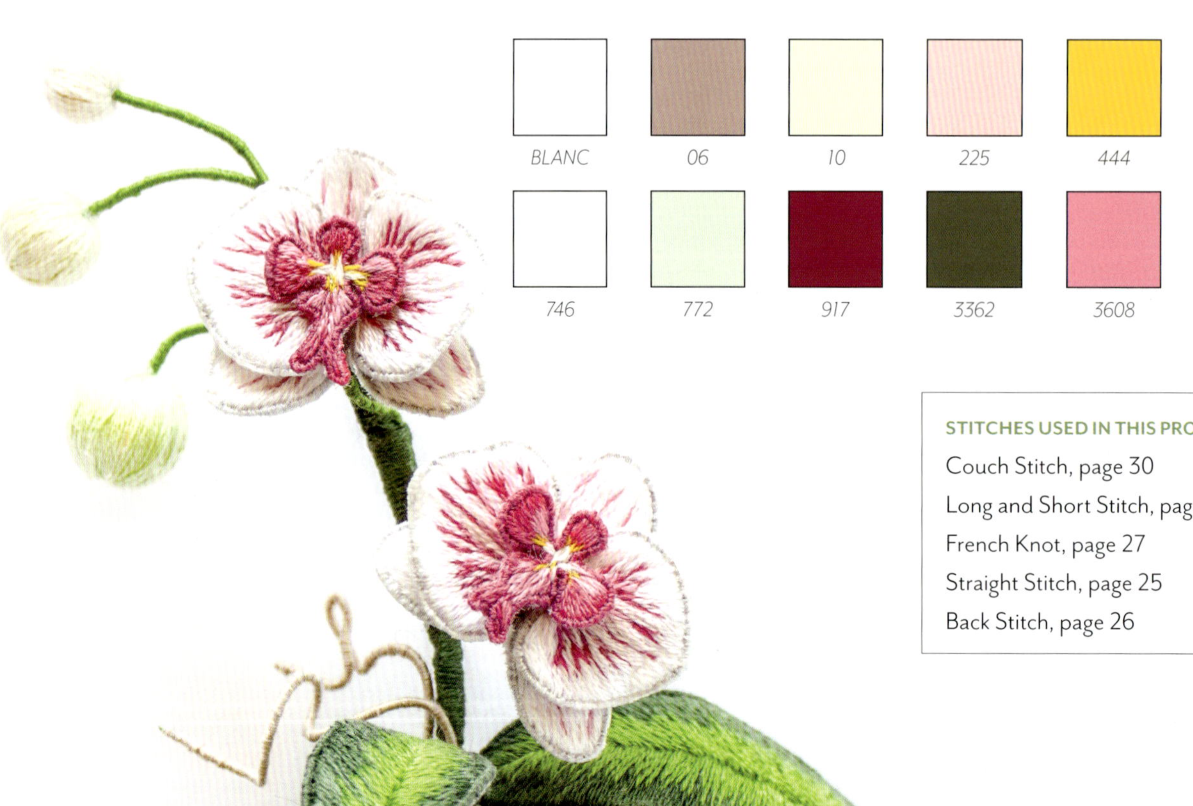

BLANC, 06, 10, 225, 444, 470, 746, 772, 917, 3362, 3608

STITCHES USED IN THIS PROJECT

- Couch Stitch, page 30
- Long and Short Stitch, page 31
- French Knot, page 27
- Straight Stitch, page 25
- Back Stitch, page 26

Transfer the Pattern

See Transferring Patterns (page 23) for more information.

1. Print or draw the Moth Orchid pattern onto the Wash-Away Stitch Stabilizer paper. Follow the printing instructions on the package. Cut out the stickers. Leave a ¼˝ (6mm) margin around each shape.

2. Secure the silk organza in the 6¼˝ (15.9cm) embroidery hoop and transfer the Moth Orchid pattern stickers to the fabric. **A**

3. Layer both squares of KONA Doeskin in the 4˝ (10.2cm) embroidery hoop.

4. Determine the size of the orchid base by tracing the diameter of your pot's opening on the fabric. **B**

Prepare the Wire Slips

See Wire Slips (page 38) for more information about wire slips. Couch the wire slips with 1 strand of DMC cotton embroidery floss and a size 10 needle.

1. Outline both pairs of petals with 30 gauge jewelry wire. Couch stitch the wire slips with DMC BLANC so the wire ends meet. **C**

2. Outline both sepals with 30 gauge jewelry wire. Couch stitch the wire slips with DMC BLANC. Twist the excess wire ends together. **D**

A

B

C

D

3. Outline the labellum with 30 gauge jewelry wire. Couch stitch the wire slips with DMC 917 so the wire ends meet. **A**

4. Outline the leaves with 24 gauge jewelry wire. Couch stitch the wire slips with DMC 3362. Twist the excess wire ends together. **B-C**

Embroider the Moss

1. Embroider the moss with French knots of The Thread Gatherer Aurora Desert Moss and a chenille needle. **D**

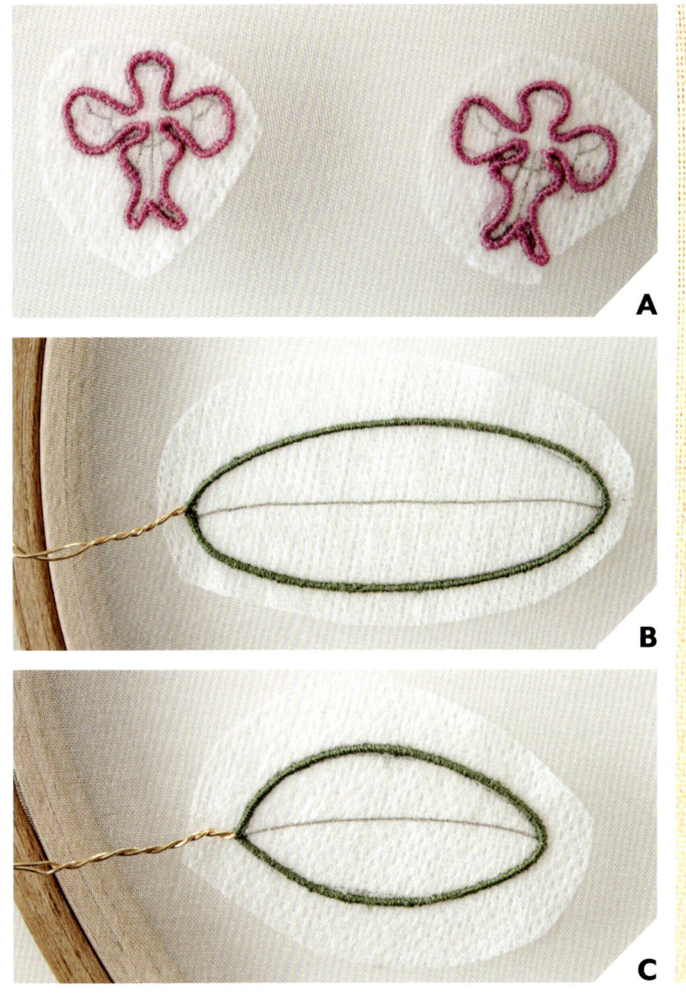
A
B
C

D

Embroider the Orchid

Embroider the orchid with 1 strand of DMC cotton embroidery thread and a size 10 embroidery needle.

Leaves

1. Begin at the inner corner of the larger leaf and embroider long and short stitches of DMC 3362 toward the center vein. Angle the stitches slightly. Blend long and short stitches of DMC 470 to fill the remaining space. **A**

2. Repeat Step 1 with the smaller leaf. **B**

Flowers

1. Backstitch the veins of the petals with DMC 3608 and 917. Fill the petals with long and short stitches of DMC BLANC and 225. **C**

2. Backstitch the veins of the sepals with DMC 3608. Begin at the center of the sepals. Fill the shape with long and short stitches of DMC BLANC. **D**

3. Embroider the labellums with long and short stitches of DMC BLANC, 444, 917, and 3608. **E**

4. Cut out the wire slips. Apply a thin layer of glue to the edges and backside of each wire slip. Let dry completely. **F**

5. Layer the orchid sepals, petals, and labellum together into 2 flowers as shown, and secure together at the center with small straight stitches of 1 strand of DMC BLANC and a size 10 embroidery needle. **G**

A B C D

E

F

G

Prepare the Thread-Wrapped Beads

See Beads (page 42) for more information about thread-wrapped beads. Wrap the beads with 2 strands of DMC cotton embroidery thread and a size 9 needle.

1. Wrap the 12mm bead with DMC 772. Wrap the 10mm bead with DMC 10. Wrap the 8mm bead with DMC 746. **A**

Prepare the Thread-Wrapped Wires

See Thread-Wrapped Wires (page 36) for more information.

1. Wrap the orchid flower stems (the twisted wire tails of the wire slips) with DMC 470. **B**

2. Cut 5 pieces of 24 gauge floral wire: 2 pieces 2½˝ (6.4cm), 1 piece 2¼˝ (5.7cm), and 2 pieces 1½˝ (3.8cm). Wrap the 2 longest wires with 1 strand of DMC 06, leaving ½˝ (1.2cm) uncovered. Wrap the 3 smaller wires completely with 1 strand of DMC 470. **C**

3. Glue the beads to the ends of the green thread-wrapped stems with fabric glue. **D**

4. Cut a 4˝ (10.2cm) piece of 2 gauge floral wire for the stem. Begin to wrap the wire with DMC 3362, attaching the smallest bud (bead and stem from Step 3) at the top, followed by the medium bud about 1cm from the top, and the largest bud about 2cm from the top.

5. Continue wrapping the stem, adding the two flowers at the 1˝ (2.5cm) and 1½˝ (3.8cm) marks from the top. Wrap the leaves and aerial roots altogether at the 2⅜˝ (6cm) mark from the top. Continue wrapping an additional ⅜˝ (1cm) of wire before tying off the end of the thread. Curl and position the aerial root wires by hand. **E**

A

B

C

D

E

Assembly

1. Create a small hole with a tapestry needle or scissors at the center of the moss, and thread the main wire of the orchid through. Flatten the excess wire against the backside of the fabric and secure the wire in place with couching stitches of DMC 3362 at the base of the stem. **A**

2. Cut a piece of mat board to fit the inside of the pot. Cut out the orchid from the fabric with a 1˝ margin. **B**

3. Thread a size 8 needle with 3 strands of DMC 470. Make a running stitch around the fabric perimeter of the mossy base. Layer a small pinch of wool roving and the mat board on the backside of the mossy base. **C**

4. Pull the ends of the running stitch threads to cinch the fabric tight around the mat board. Tighten the fabric on the backside of the embroidery by lacing the excess thread back and forth across the fabric. **D**

5. Fit the embroidery into the pot. Secure in place with super glue if needed.

A

B

C

D

Venus Fly Trap

FINISHED PROJECT SIZE: 2½˝ × 3˝ (6.4 × 7.6cm)

Although venus fly traps are native to only a small area of the United States, they are widely recognizable for their unusual appearance and diet. I have tried repeatedly and unsuccessfully to keep one as a houseplant, but they proved too difficult for my inexperience and not-so-green thumb. Instead, I have embroidered one that will stay green perpetually. This pattern showcases the plant's bright colors, stitched with thread painting, and detailed wire slips to recreate their iconic traps.

Materials

4˝(10.2cm) embroidery hoop

Size 10 embroidery needle

Tapestry needle

Thread conditioner

30 gauge jewelry wire

Wire cutters

Small, pointed scissors

Fabric glue

Craft-quality detail paint brush

Venus Fly Trap Base pattern (page 158)

Venus Fly Trap Wireslips pattern (page 158)

Frame or display hoop, optional

Fabric and Thread

2 squares 6˝ × 6˝(15.2 × 15.2cm) of KONA cotton in Cerise

6˝ × 6˝ square (15.2 × 15.2cm) of KONA cotton in Cactus

1 skein each of the following DMC 6-stranded cotton embroidery floss colors

STITCHES USED IN THIS PROJECT

Couch Stitch, page 30

Long and Short Stitch, page 31

Transfer the Pattern

See Transferring Patterns (page 23) for more information.

1. Transfer the Venus Fly Trap Wireslips pattern to a square of KONA cotton Cactus using your preferred method. I used black graphite transfer paper. Secure in the 4˝ (10.2cm) embroidery hoop. **A**

2. Transfer the Venus Fly Trap Base pattern to the KONA cotton Cerise using your preferred method. I used white graphite paper. **B**

Prepare the Wire Slips

See Wire Slips (page 38) for more information about wire slips. Embroider the wire slips with a size 10 needle and 1 strand of DMC cotton embroidery thread.

1. Outline the open venus fly trap with 30 gauge wire, and couch in place with DMC 10 and 703 as shown with the wire ends twisted.

2. Outline the trap halves with 30 gauge wire, and couch in place with DMC 10 and 701 as shown. **C**

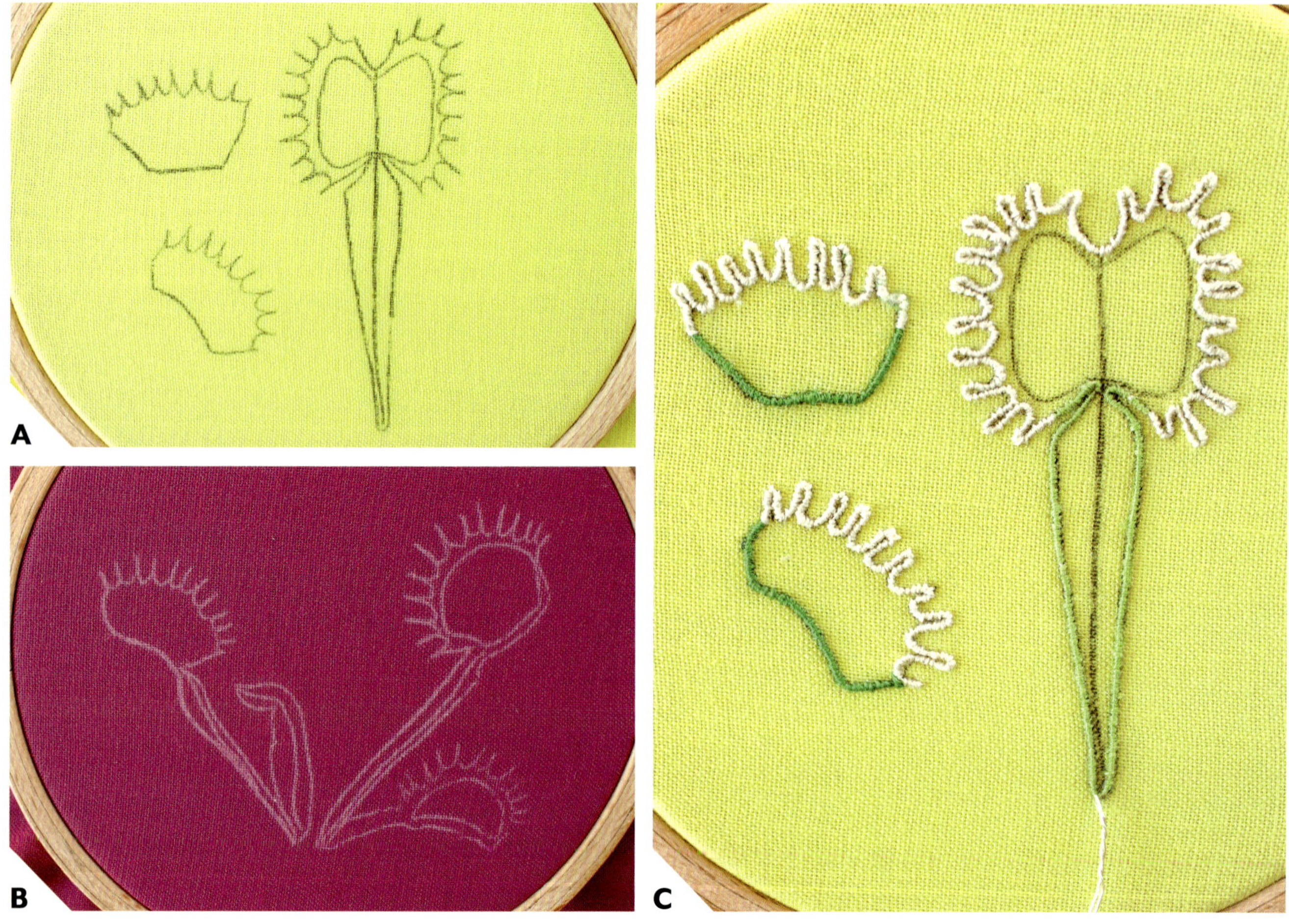
A
B
C

Embroider the Wire Slips

Embroider the wire slips with a size 10 needle and 1 strand of DMC cotton embroidery thread.

1. Begin at the the center of the open trap and blend long and short stitches of DMC 3777, 22, and 3722 to create a gradient from dark to light red. Angle the stitches slightly so they radiate outward to the spines. Fill in the rest of the spines with long and short stitches of DMC 704, 15, and 10. Fill in the base of the trap with long and short stitches of 703 with a line of 701 along the center vein. **A**

2. Begin at the bottom of the trap halves. Blend long and short stitches of DMC 701, 704, 16, and 15 (in that order) to fill the trap with an ombre effect of dark green to light green. Add straight stitches of DMC 10 to each spine. **B-C**

Embroider the Venus Fly Trap

Embroider the venus fly trap with a size 10 needle and 1 strand of DMC cotton embroidery thread.

1. Secure both layers of the KONA Cerise fabric in the hoop. Embroider the stems with long and short stitches of DMC 701, 703, and 704. **D**

2. Embroider the closed trap with long and short stitches of DMC 701, 704, 16, 15, and 10. **E**

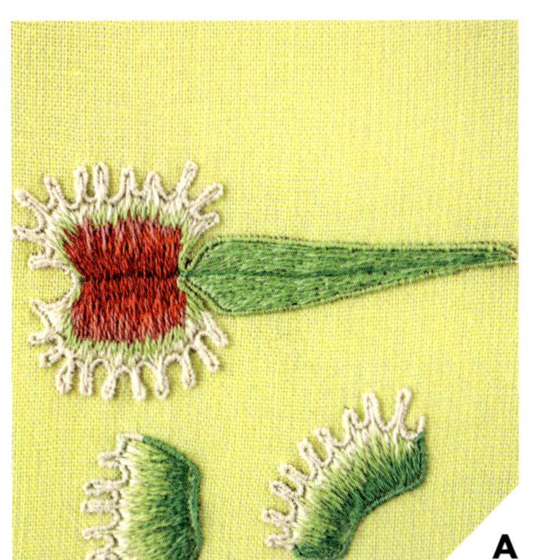
A

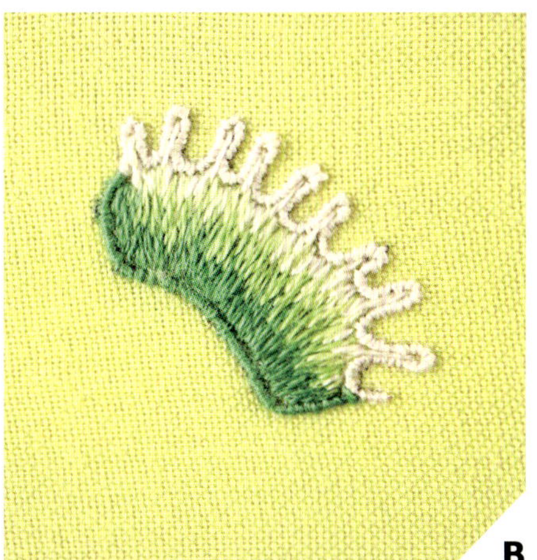
B

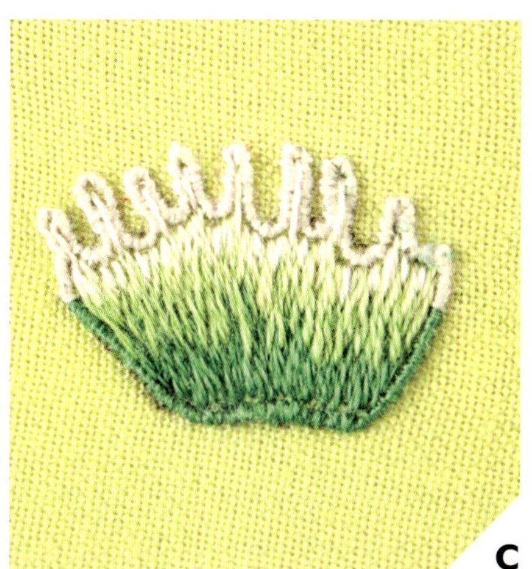
C

D

E

3. Begin at the flat edge of the open trap. Blend long and short stitches of DMC 3777, 22, and 3722 (in that order) to create a gradient of dark to light red and fill the center of the trap up to 2mm below the spines. Fill in the rest of the trap with a dark to light green gradient of long and short stitches of DMC 704, 16, and 15 (in that order). Add straight stitches of DMC 10 to embroider each spine. **A-B**

A

B

Assembly

See Wire Slips (page 38).

1. Cut out the wire slips. Carefully apply glue to the edges and backside of the traps with fabric glue and a paint brush. **C**

• CUTTING AROUND DETAILED WIRE SLIPS •

Use very precise scissors, such as Karen Kay Buckley's 4˝ Perfect scissors, to carefully cut around the scalloped edges of each fly trap wire slip. Glue the edges and use needle-nose tweezers to help shape the scalloped edges on the traps and fold back any excess fabric from the edges.

C

2. Use a tapestry needle to make a hole for the open trap wire slip in the middle of the pattern. Attach it to the Cerise fabric with couch stitches at its base with DMC 701 and a size 10 needle. Align the 1˝ (2.5cm) wide trap wireslip with the bottom right fly trap and the ¾˝ (1.9cm) wide trap wireslip with the upper right fly trap. Secure each trap half in place with couch stitches of DMC 701 along the bottom edge of the wireslip. **D**

3. See Displaying Embroidery (page 16) for instructions on how to secure your fly trap in a hoop or frame. I transferred mine to a round frame with a matching color palette.

D

Amanita Mushroom

FINISHED PROJECT SIZE: 3½˝ × 4˝ (8.9 × 10.2cm)

The poisonous Amanita mushroom is easily identified by its vibrant red and orange cap that serves as a warning to any would-be predator. I love how these beautiful mushrooms bring unexpectedly vivid color to a forest floor. They stand apart from the earth tones of fallen leaves and sticks. This pattern creates a life-like replica complete with a skeletal leaf, moss, and dew drops. Display it as a terrarium in a glass cloche dome for a captivating finish.

Materials

7½˝ (19.1cm) and 4˝ (10.2cm) embroidery hoops

Size 10 embroidery needle

Size 10 beading needle

Size 18 Chenille needle

Scissors

Fabric glue

Super glue

Watercolor paints or other painting medium

Large mop or round watercolor paint brush

Benzie Design Corriedale wool roving: Fern

38 Gauge Cross Star felting needle

Needle felting pad

Soldering iron with rounded tip (optional)

2 tapered corks 1˝ long

6/0 Czech clear iridescent glass beads

11/0 Miyuki Rocailles clear glass beads

C&T Publishing Wash-Away Stitch Stabilizer paper

Graphite tracing paper (white)

Amanita Mushroom pattern (page 156)

Moss pattern (page 157)

Skeletal Leaf pattern (page 157)

Mat board

Glass Cloche display (optional)

Fabric and Thread

10˝ × 10˝ (25.4 × 25.4cm) square of silk organza

2 squares 7˝ × 7˝ (17.8 × 17.8cm) of KONA cotton in Kelly

6˝ × 6˝ (15.2cm × 15.2cm) square of C&T Publishing Lutradur Mixed Media sheet

Rainbow Gallery Fluffy Fleece #2

The Thread Gatherer:

- Silken Pearl #058 Strawflower
- Sea Grass thread in #144 Green Leaves
- Aurora thread in #031 Woods of Gold
- Aurora thread in #015 Olive Branch
- Sanibel thread in #024 Mississippi Mud
- LaBrume thread #020 In the Pines
- Silken Pearl size 5 #060 Burnished Gold

DMC 6-stranded variegated cotton embroidery floss #4045

DMC wool tapestry yarn #7364

1 skein each of the following DMC 6-stranded cotton embroidery floss colors

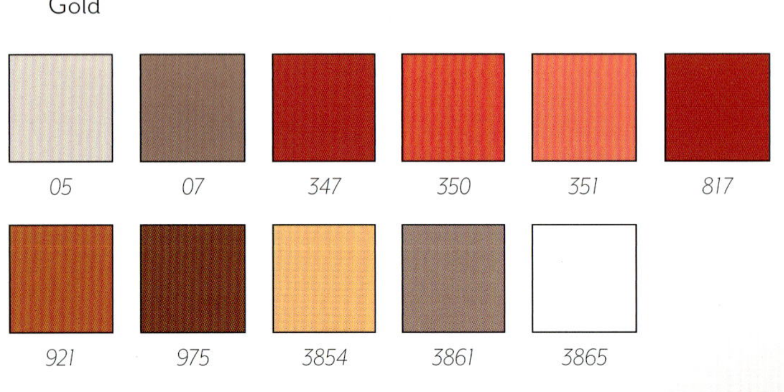

STITCHES USED IN THIS PROJECT

Back Stitch, page 26

Long and Short Stitch, page 31

French Knot, page 27

Turkey Stitch, page 29

Seed Stitch, page 25

Straight Stitch, page 25

Couch Stitch, page 30

Transfer the Pattern

See Transferring Patterns (page 23) for more information.

1. Secure the silk organza in the 7½˝ (19.1cm) embroidery hoop. Transfer the Amanita Mushroom pattern to the fabric with the stitch stabilizer paper. **A**

2. Secure both 7˝ (17.8cm) squares of KONA Kelly together in the 4˝ (10.2cm) embroidery hoop. Transfer the Moss pattern to the center of the hoop using your preferred method. I used a white graphite paper. **B**

3. Paint the sheet of Lutradur using your preferred medium in colors for the skeletal autumn leaf. I used watercolor paints and water-soluble pastels in shades of deep purple, burgundy, dark brown, and ochre yellow. **C**

4. Transfer the Skeletal Leaf pattern to the sheet of Lutradur with a pencil or heat-erasable pen.

Prepare the Padded Base

See Needle-Felted Padding (page 34) for more information about felted padding.

1. Felt the Moss pattern with the Fern green Corriedale roving and 38 gauge star-tipped felting needle. Fill the circle entirely. Felt more wool as needed to make the padding stand about 1˝ (2.5cm) tall. The padded shape should be evenly rounded and firm. **D**

Make the Skeletal Leaf

1. Secure the leaf pattern in the 4" (10.2cm) hoop. Back stitch the veins of the leaf with a size 10 needle and 1 strand of DMC 975. Do not trail your thread across the backside from vein to vein to avoid visible threads showing through. Instead, start a new thread at the beginning of each vein. **A-B**

2. Cut out the leaf. Be careful to not cut into the vein stitching. **C**

3. Set the soldering iron to 300 degrees. Carefully burn away the edges and make small holes throughout the leaf. Do not burn too close to the stitching or it will unravel. **D**

• SOLDERING IRON ALTERNATIVES •

A soldering iron is my preferred tool for this technique because it creates a unique and realistic effect. If you are uncomfortable using a soldering iron or do not have access to one, you can achieve a similar look with small and precise scissors, such as Karen Kay Buckley's Perfect 4" scissors. Cut away the edges unevenly, leaving ragged and torn fibers. You can also use pointed tools, such as a toothpick, to poke holes in the lutradur to recreate the skeletal leaf's decaying look.

A

B

C

D

Make the Mushroom

Embroider the mushroom with 1 strand of DMC cotton embroidery thread and a size 10 needle unless otherwise specified.

Embroider the Cap

1. The larger circle is the top of the mushroom cap. Beginning at the center, stitch out toward the edges of the cap, angling the stitches. Fill the cap with long and short stitches of DMC 347, 817, 350, 351, 921, and 3854, going from red to orange. **A**

2. Add a random pattern of seed stitches and French knots to the cap with 3 strands of DMC 3865 and a size 8 needle. Wrap the thread around the needle 1 to 4 times to create a variety of French knot sizes. **B**

Embroider the Gills

1. The smaller circle pattern is the underside of the mushroom cap, or the gills. Blend long and short stitches of DMC 05, 07, and 3861 to fill the gills of the mushroom, going from dark to light (center to edges). **C**

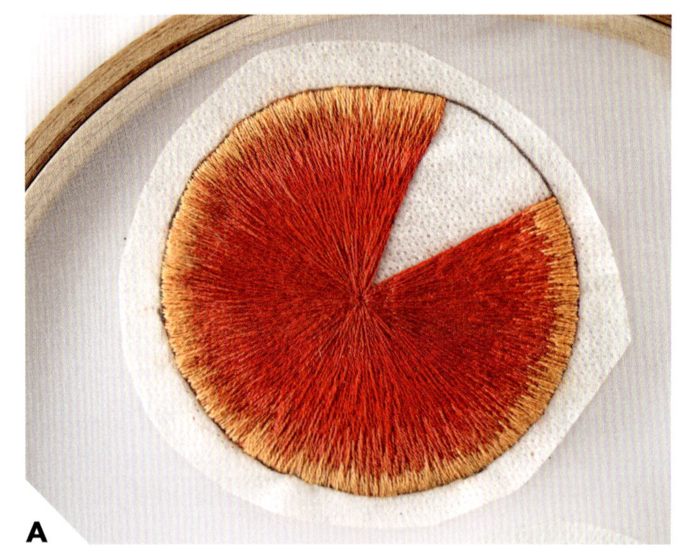

A

B

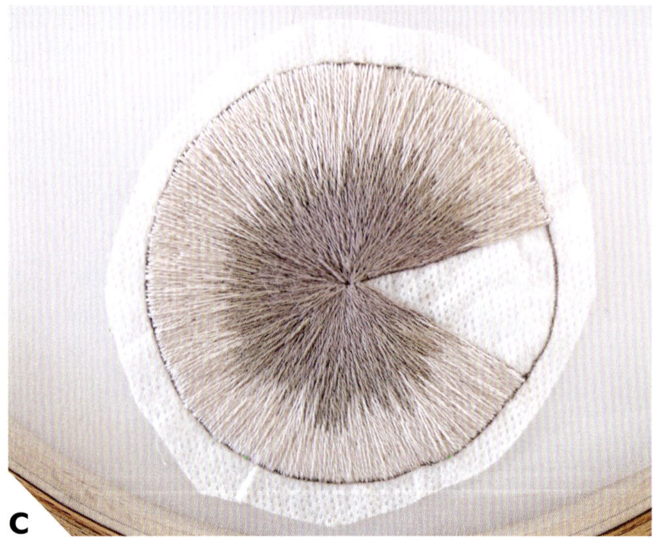

C

Assemble the Cap

1. Cut around the top of the mushroom cap leaving a ⅜″ (1cm) margin of fabric. Make slits along the excess fabric. **A**

2. Where there is an unstitched wedge, cut a slit alongside one inner edge of stitching. **B**

3. Fold the excess fabric over to the back of the mushroom cap, and adhere in place with fabric glue. **C**

4. Bring the two inner edges of the cap together, joining the stitching, and adhere in place with fabric glue. **D**

5. Repeat Steps 1–4 with the gills (underside of the gap). **E**

A

B

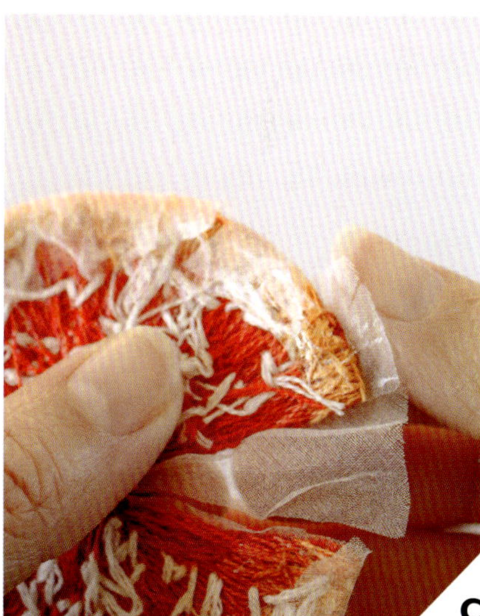

C

D

E

6. Glue the gills to the underside of the cap. **F**

7. Thread a size 10 needle with 1 strand of DMC 3854. Begin on the gill side of the cap and bring the needle through both layers. **G**

8. Bring the needle back around to the gills, then through the mushroom again (from gills to cap) to create a loop of thread around the edge of the cap that is about 5mm from the edge. Start the next stitch directly next to the first loop. **H**

9. Continue to embroider the edge around the cap until it is completely covered. **I**

F

G

H

I

Make the Stalk

See Wires (page 36) for more information. Apply the thread-wrapped wire technique to the cork bottle stoppers in Steps 1–4.

1. Place The Thread Gatherer Silken Pearl #058 Strawflower thread alongside the cork. **A**

2. Begin at the narrow end and wrap the thread around the cork, careful not to overlap the thread at any point so the thread is one smooth layer. **B**

3. Secure the thread at the end of the cork with a dab of fabric glue. **C**

4. Repeat Steps 1–3 with the other cork. **D**

5. Stack and glue the two thread-wrapped corks together with super glue to form the mushroom stalk as shown. Glue the stalk to the center of the gills. **E**

6. Glue the Rainbow Gallery Fluffy Fleece #2 around the center of the stalk where the two corks meet with fabric glue. **F**

Attach the Mushroom

1. Insert a 5˝ (12.7cm) piece of floral wire at the base of the mushroom stalk about 1˝ (2.5cm) deep. **A**

2. Transfer the felted circle back into the 4˝ (10.2cm) hoop. Insert the wire into the center of the felted fabric base and couch stitch the wire in place. Curl the wire so that it lays flat against the backside of the fabric and couch stitch to anchor it in place on the backside. **B**

A

Embroider the Moss

Use a chenille needle to embroider the moss. The thread numbers refer to The Thread Gatherer threads, unless otherwise specified.

1. Begin to embroider over the felted base with small (2–3cm) irregular-shaped areas of straight stitches and French knots. Use #031 Woods of Gold, #015 Olive Branch, #020 In the Pines, #060 Burnished Gold, and DMC #7364. Cover about half of the padded base. Leave gaps in between the areas of French knots to be filled with turkey stitches in Step 2.

2. Fill in the remaining gaps with sections of turkey stitches. Use #144 Green Leaves, #024 Mississippi Mud, DMC #4045, and #7364. Trim the turkey stitches to various lengths to create different textures. Leave the sea grass thread long (2cm), to mimic grass.

B

· EMBROIDERING REALISTIC MOSS ·

The key to embroidering vibrant and realistic-looking moss is to greatly vary the fibers and stitches you use. If you do not have these specific threads, you can substitute other green, gold, and brown threads to achieve a similar look. Explore different types of fibers, such as silk, wool, chenille, and linen. They will each have a unique look when stitched with French knots, turkey stitches, and even straight stitches, much like real moss varieties.

3. Thread a beading needle with 1 strand of DMC 3865. Embroider clear crystal seed beads to the moss to mimic dew drops. **C**

4. Couch stitch the skeletal leaf to the moss with DMC 975.

C

Finishing

See Displaying in a Frame (page 16) for more information.

1. Cut a 2¼″ (5.7cm) circle from the mat board. Cut away the excess fabric, leaving a 1″ (2.5cm) margin around the moss base.

2. Make a running stitch around the fabric perimeter of the mossy base. Layer a pinch of wool roving and the mat board on the base of the fabric, then pull the ends of the running stitch threads to cinch the fabric tight around the mat board. Tighten the fabric on the backside of the embroidery by lacing the excess thread back and forth across the fabric. **A**

3. Attach the matt board to the wooden display base with super glue.

A

TEMPLATES

To access the patterns as a digital download, scan this QR code

or go to tinyurl.com/11645-patterns-download

IO MOTH BODY

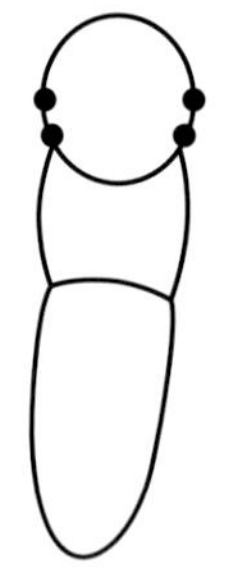

IO MOTH WINGS

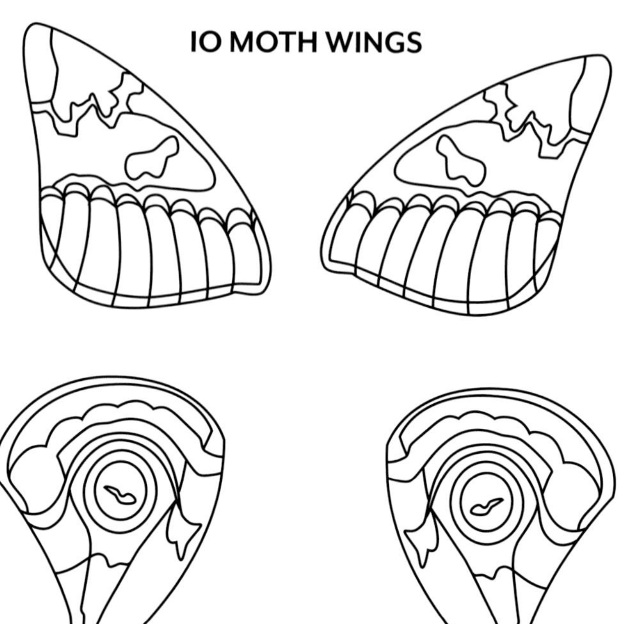

FROG TOPSIDE

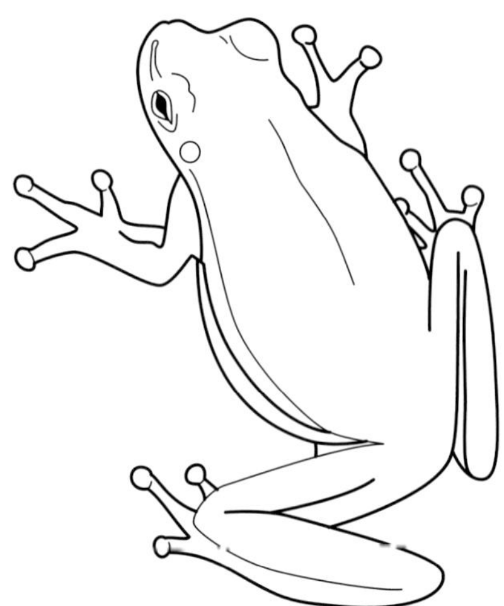

FROG UNDERSIDE

HEDGEHOG

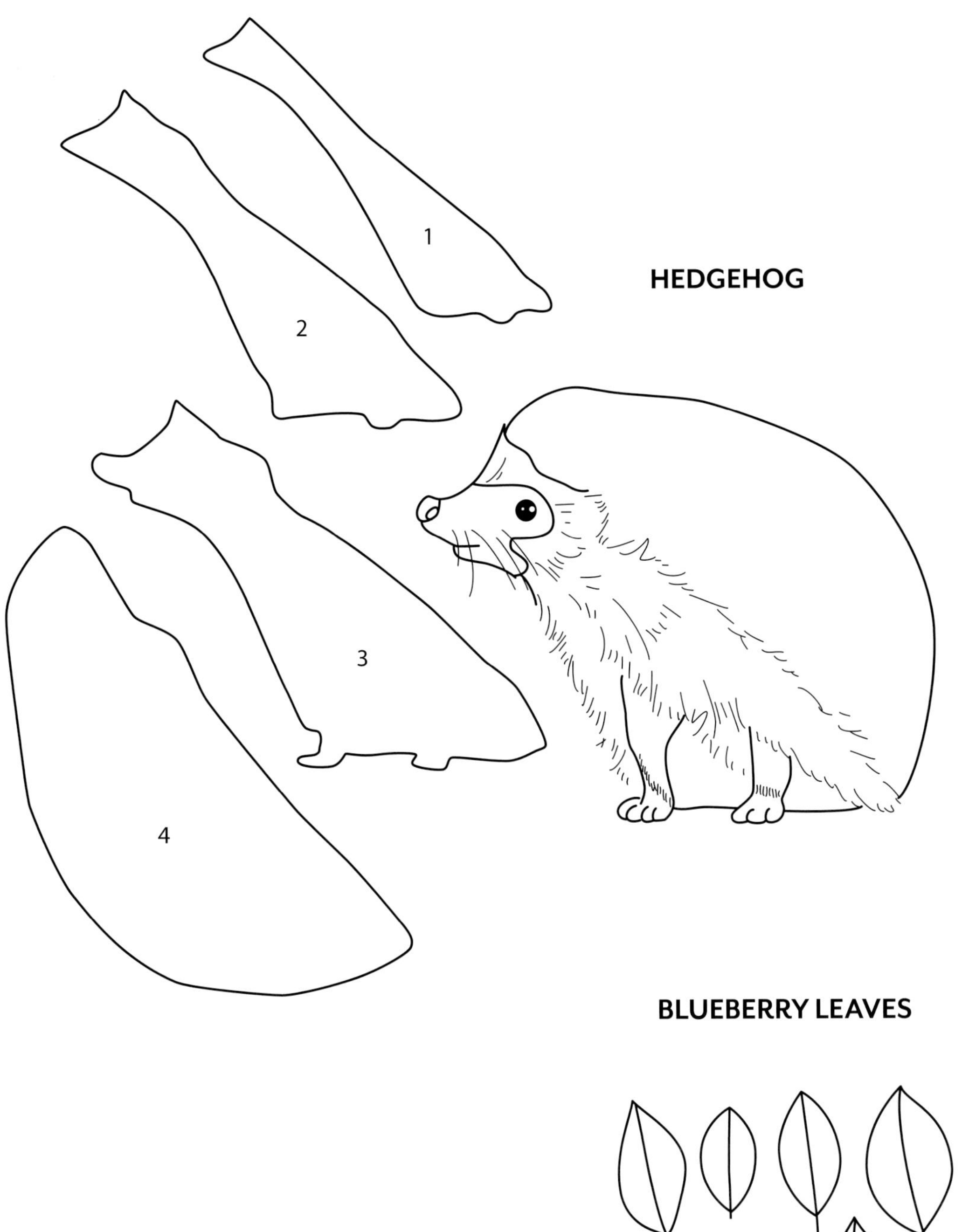

BLUEBERRY LEAVES

SPIDERWEB

LARGE BLACKBERRY

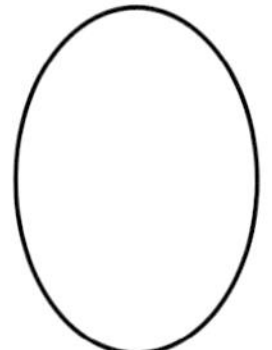

SMALL BLACKBERRY

BLACKBERRY LEAVES

RIVER OTTER

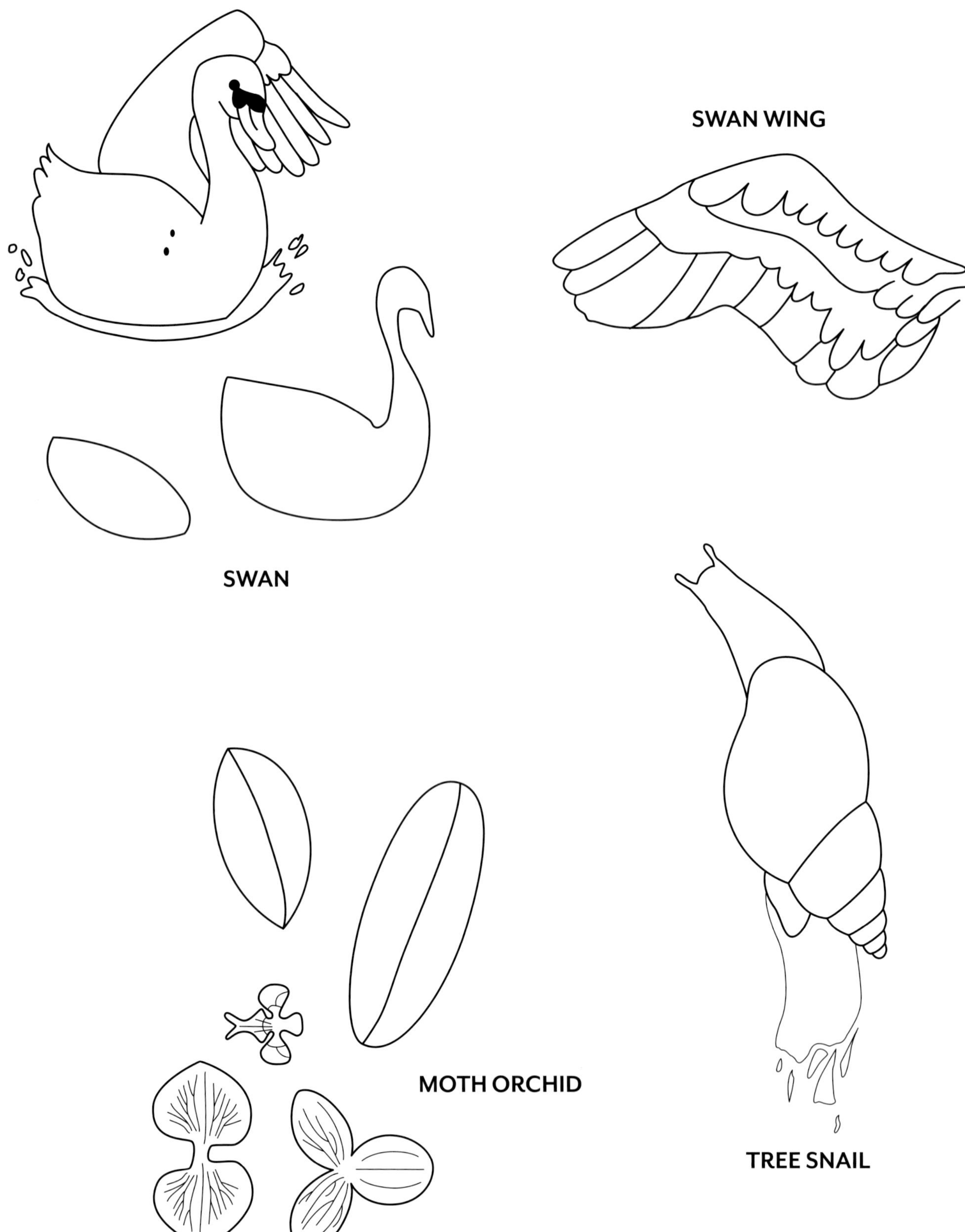
SWAN WING
SWAN
MOTH ORCHID
TREE SNAIL

OLD WORLD SWALLOWTAIL BODY

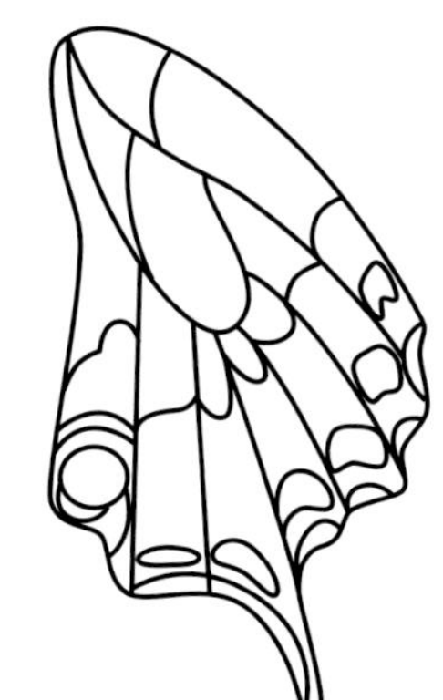

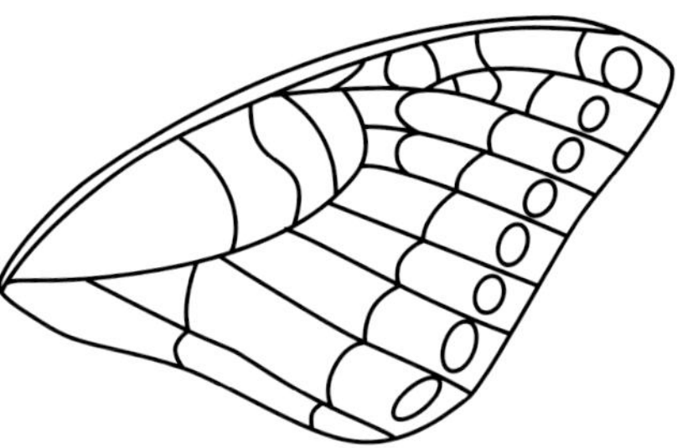

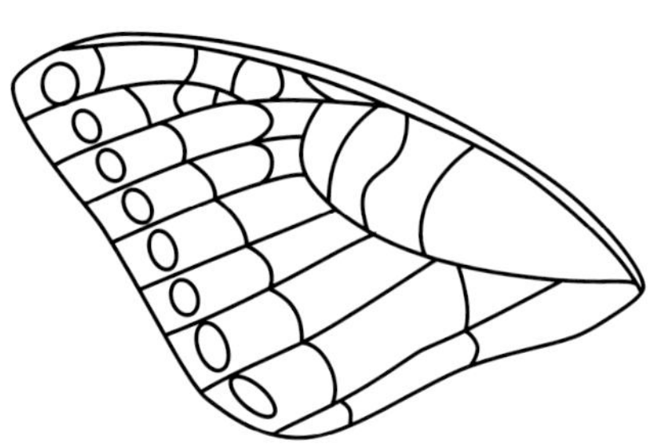

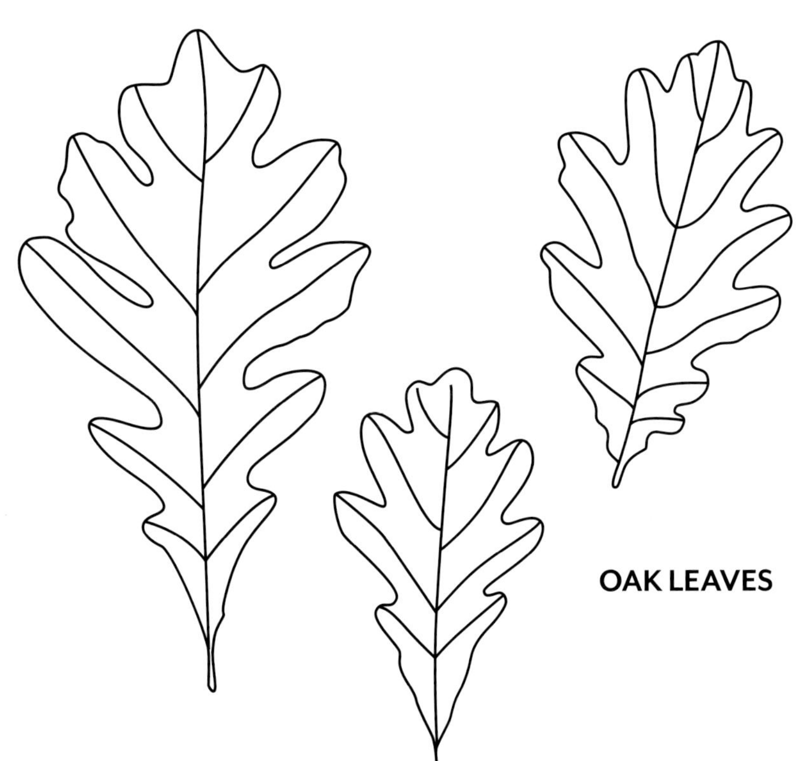

OAK LEAVES

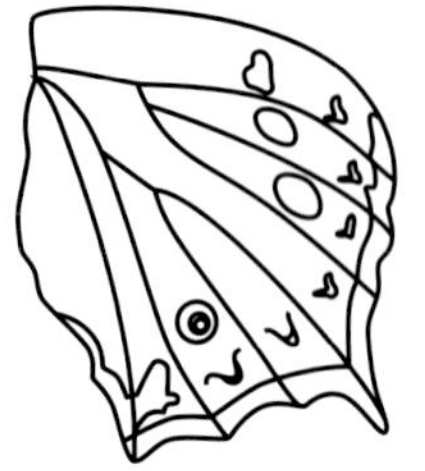
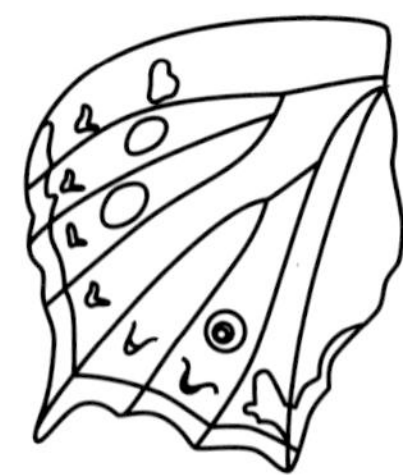
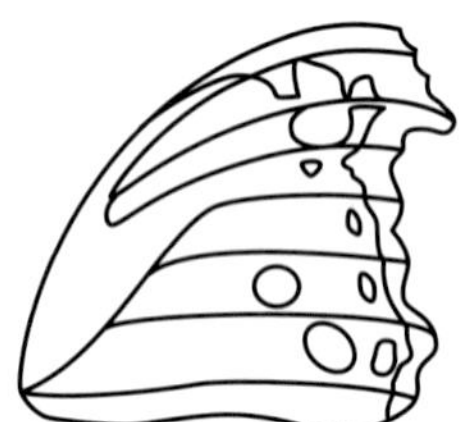
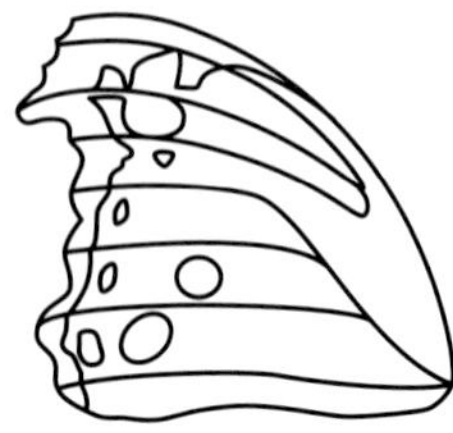

FOREST MOTHER
OF PEARL WINGS

AMANITA
MUSHROOM

FOREST MOTHER
OF PEARL BODY

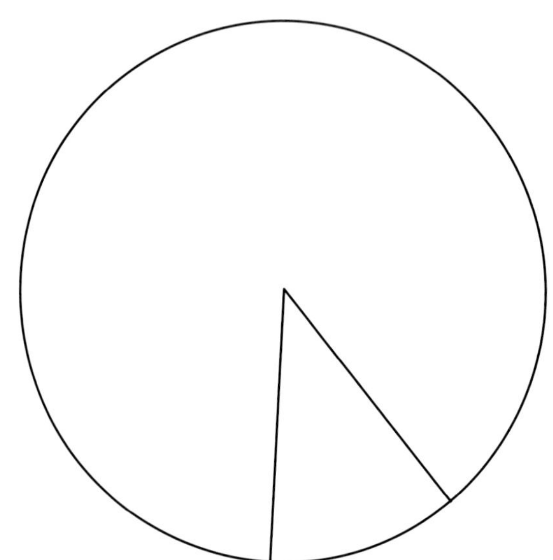

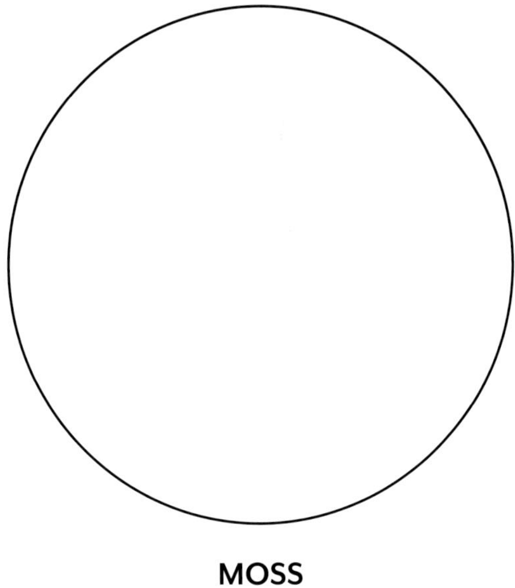

MOSS

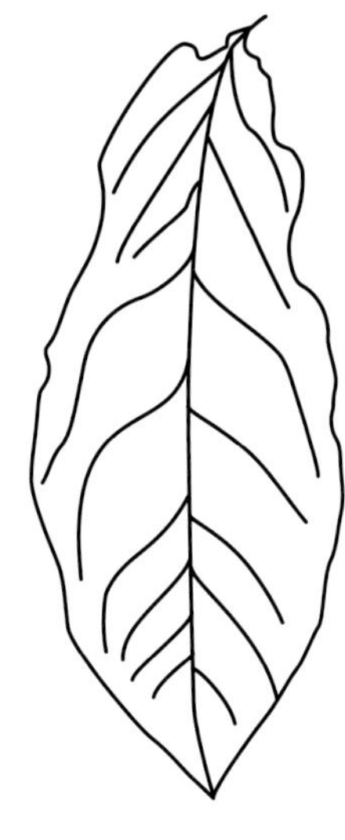

SKELETAL LEAF

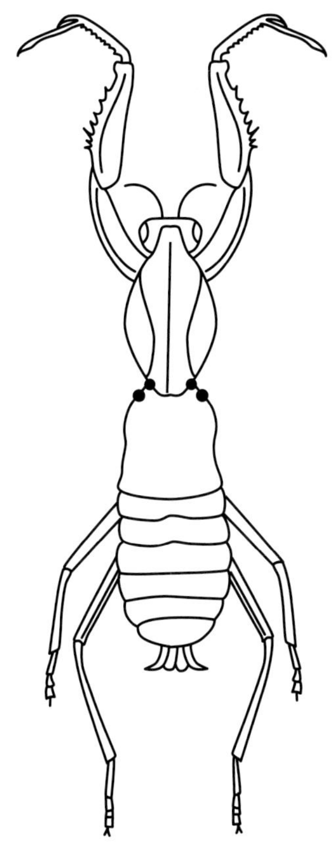

PRAYING MANTIS BODY

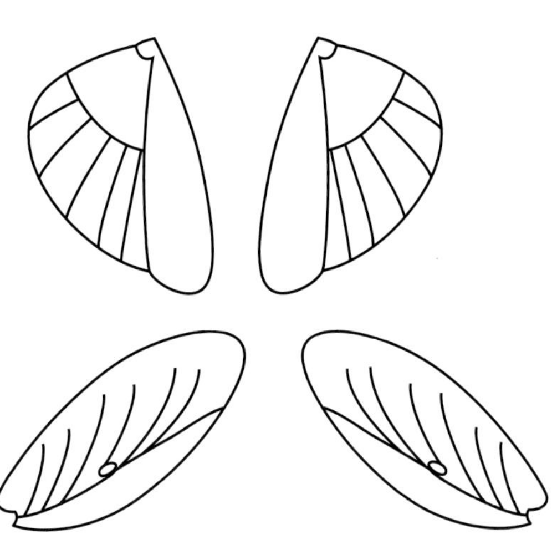

PRAYING MANTIS
WINGS

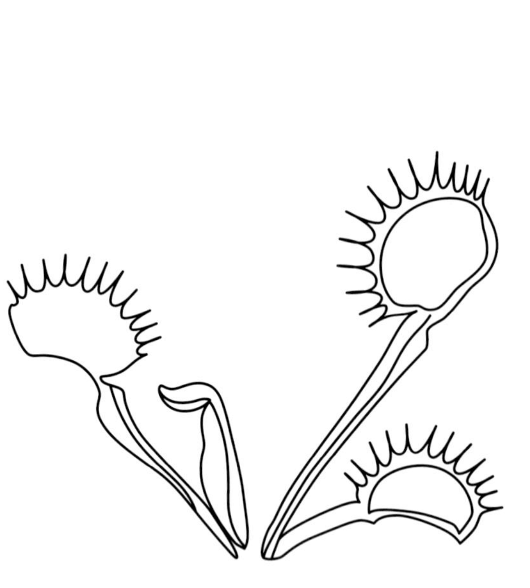

VENUS FLY TRAP BASE

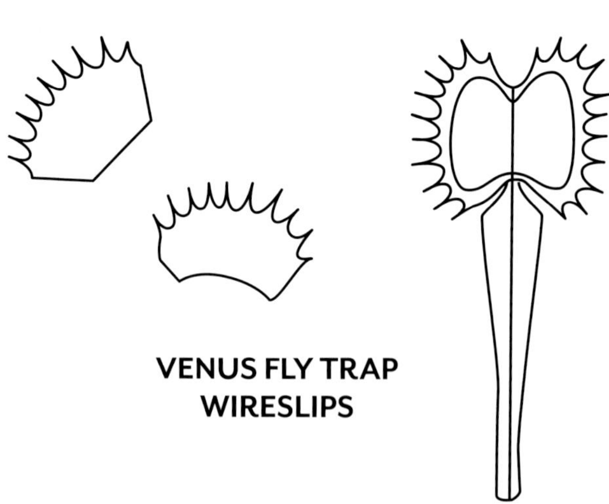

VENUS FLY TRAP WIRESLIPS

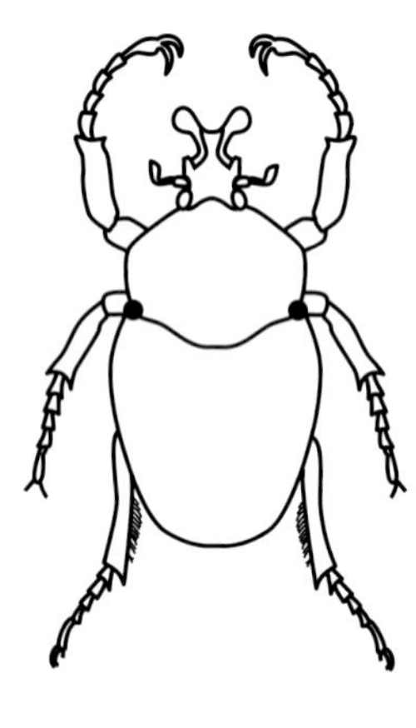

BEETLE BODY

BEETLE WINGS

BEETLE THORAX

BEETLE WING CASINGS

ABOUT THE AUTHOR

Megan Zaniewski is a San Antonio, TX based author and artist whose work is inspired by the quiet beauty of nature, brought to life in her intricate three-dimensional embroidery. She spends her days homeschooling her three children and finds time to stitch between the rhythms of family life. Her work is often inspired by small, everyday observations of the flora and fauna found just outside her door, as well as her children's contagious curiosity of the natural world. She has authored two books and has appeared in numerous publications and exhibitions worldwide. You can follow her embroidery work on Instagram **@megembroiders**

CREATIVE

SPARK

ONLINE LEARNING

Quilting courses to become an expert quilter...

From their studio to yours, Creative Spark instructors are teaching you how to create and become a master of your craft. So not only do you get a look inside their creative space, you also get to be a part of engaging courses that would typically be a one or multi-day workshop from the comfort of your home.

Creative Spark is not your one-size-fits-all online learning experience. We welcome you to be who you are, share, create, and belong.

Scan for a gift from us!

creativespark.ctpub.com